DATE DUE

FEB 11 1988		
18 MAY 1988		
APR 28 1990		
FEB 8 1991		

DEMCO 38-296

An American National Standard

IEEE Standards for
Local Area Networks:

Token Ring Access Method and
Physical Layer Specifications

Published by
The Institute of Electrical and Electronics Engineers, Inc

Distributed in cooperation with
Wiley-Interscience, a division of John Wiley & Sons, Inc

ANSI/IEEE Std 802.5-1985
ISO Draft
Proposal
8802/5

An American National Standard

IEEE Standards for Local Area Networks:

Token Ring Access Method and Physical Layer Specifications

Sponsor

**Technical Committee Computer Communications
of the
IEEE Computer Society**

Approved December 13, 1984

IEEE Standards Board

Approved March 19, 1985

American National Standards Institute

ISBN 0-471-82996-X

Library of Congress Catalog Number 85-060360

© Copyright 1985 by

The Institute of Electrical and Electronics Engineers, Inc
345 East 47th Street, New York, NY 10017, USA

April 29, 1985   *SH09944*

Foreword

(This Foreword is not a part of ANSI/IEEE Std 802.5-1985, Token Ring Access Method and Physical Layer Specifications.)

This standard is part of a family of standards for Local Area Networks (LANs). The relationship between this standard and the other members of the family is shown below. (The numbers in the figure refer to IEEE Standard numbers.)

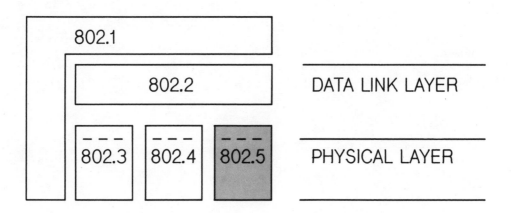

This family of standards deals with the physical and data link layers as defined by the ISO Open Systems Interconnection Reference Model. The access standards define three types of medium access technologies and associated physical media, each appropriate for particular applications or system objectives. The standards defining these technologies are:

1) ANSI/IEEE Std 802.3-1985 (ISO DIS 8802/3), a bus utilizing CSMA/CD as the access method

2) ANSI/IEEE Std 802.4-1985 (ISO DIS 8802/4), a bus utilizing token passing as the access method

3) ANSI/IEEE Std 802.5-1985 (ISO DP 8802/5), a ring utilizing token passing as the access method

Other access methods (for example, metropolitan area networks) are under investigation.

ANSI/IEEE Std 802.2-1985 (ISO DIS 8802/2), Logical Link Control protocol, is used in conjunction with the medium access standards.

A companion document, IEEE 802.1,[1] describes the relationship among these standards and their relationship to the ISO Open Systems Interconnection Reference Model in more detail. This companion document will contain internetworking and network management issues.

The reader of this document is urged to become familiar with the complete family of standards.

NOTE: This ANSI/IEEE Std 802.5-1985 specifies that each octet of the information field shall be transmitted most significant bit (MSB) first. This convention is reversed from that used in the ANSI/IEEE Std 802.3-1985 and ANSI/IEEE Std 802.4-1985 standards which are Least Significant Bit (LSB) first transmission. While the transmission of MSB first is used for the ANSI/IEEE 802.5-1985 token ring, this does not imply that MSB transmission is preferable for any other type of local area network. Anyone considering the interconnection of the ANSI/IEEE 802.5-1985 token ring with other IEEE standard networks should keep in mind the need to perform bit reordering in the gateway between networks.

---

[1]In preparation.

Voting members of the 802.5 Working Group who participated in developing this standard were as follows:

Robert A. Donnan, *Chairman*

H. Abramowicz
A. Philip Arneth
Nichlos Beale
Charles Brill
Werner Bux
Guy Crauwels
R. W. Gibson
Fred Greim
Robert Grow
Tom Gulick
Lee C. Haas
Nobuhiro Hamada
Lloyd Hasley
Tetsuo Isayama
Jiro Kashio
Makoto Kohno

Stan Kopec
Robert Krebs
Eiji Kuge
David Laffitte
Laurie Lindsey
Robert D. Love
Narayan Murthy
Shigekatsu Nakao
W. B. Neblett
James Nelson
Michael W. Patrick
John Rance
Everett O. Rigsbee
Robert Rosenthal
Floyd Ross
Don Roworth
Howard C. Salwen

W. L. Schumacher
Tim Shafer
Naoshi Shima
D. T. W. Sze
V. Tarassov
Nathan Tobol
Art Torino
Bo Viklund
John Q. Walker
Frank Wang
Ian Watson
R. O. Westlake
Albert Wong
Howard D. Wright
H. A. Zannini
Mo Zonoun

When the IEEE Standards Board approved this standard on December 13, 1984, it had the following membership:

James H. Beall, *Chairman*   **John E. May,** *Vice Chairman*
Sava I. Sherr, *Secretary*

J. J. Archambault
John T. Boettger
J. V. Bonucchi
Rene Castenschiold
Edward J. Cohen
Len S. Corey
Donald C. Fleckenstein
Jay Forster

Daniel L. Goldberg
Donald N. Heirman
Irvin N. Howell
Jack Kinn
Joseph L. Koepfinger*
Irving Kolodny
George Konomos
R. F. Lawrence

Donald T. Michael*
John P. Riganati
Frank L. Rose
Robert W. Seelbach
Jay A. Stewart
Clifford O. Swanson
W. B. Wilkens
Charles J. Wylie

*Member emeritus

Contents

SECTION   PAGE

1. General   19
   1.1 Scope   19
   1.2 Definitions   20

2. General Description   23

3. Formats and Facilities   27
   3.1 Formats   27
       3.1.1 Token Format   27
       3.1.2 Frame Format   27
       3.1.3 Fill   28
   3.2 Field Descriptions   28
       3.2.1 Starting Delimiter (SD)   28
       3.2.2 Access Control (AC)   28
       3.2.3 Frame Control (FC)   29
       3.2.4 Destination and Source Address Fields   30
       3.2.5 Information (INFO) Field   31
       3.2.6 Frame Check Sequence (FCS)   33
       3.2.7 Ending Delimiter (ED)   34
       3.2.8 Frame Status (FS)   34
   3.3 MAC Frames   35
       3.3.1 Claim Token MAC Frame (CL—TK)   35
       3.3.2 Duplicate Address Test MAC Frame (DAT)   36
       3.3.3 Active Monitor Present MAC Frame (AMP)   36
       3.3.4 Standby Monitor Present MAC Frame (SMP)   36
       3.3.5 Beacon MAC Frame (BCN)   37
       3.3.6 Purge MAC Frame (PRG)   37
   3.4 Timers   38
       3.4.1 Timer, Return to Repeat (TRR)   38
       3.4.2 Timer, Holding Token (THT)   38
       3.4.3 Timer, Queue PDU (TQP)   38
       3.4.4 Timer, Valid Transmission (TVX)   38
       3.4.5 Timer, No Token (TNT)   38
       3.4.6 Timer, Active Monitor (TAM)   39
       3.4.7 Timer, Standby Monitor (TSM)   39
   3.5 Flags   39
   3.6 Priority Registers and Stacks   39
   3.7 Latency Buffer   39

4. Token Ring Protocols   41
   4.1 Overview   41
       4.1.1 Frame Transmission   41
       4.1.2 Token Transmission   41
       4.1.3 Stripping   41

       4.1.4 Frame Reception..................................... 41
       4.1.5 Priority Operation 42
       4.1.6 Beaconing and Neighbor Notification 43
   4.2 Specification....................................... 45
       4.2.1 Receive Actions..................................... 47
       4.2.2 Operational Finite-State Machine....................... 49
       4.2.3 Standby Monitor Finite-State Machine 53
       4.2.4 Active Monitor Finite-State Machine 57

5. Service Specifications 59
   5.1 MAC to LLC Service 59
       5.1.1 Interactions 59
       5.1.2 Detailed Service Specifications........................ 59
   5.2 PHY to MAC Service 62
       5.2.1 Interactions 62
       5.2.2 Detailed Service Specifications........................ 62
   5.3 MAC to NMT Service 64
       5.3.1 Interactions 64
       5.3.2 Detailed Service Specifications........................ 64
   5.4 PHY to NMT Service 70
       5.4.1 Interactions 70
       5.4.2 Detailed Service Specifications........................ 70

6. Physical Layer 73
   6.1 Symbol Encoding 73
   6.2 Symbol Decoding 74
   6.3 Data Signalling Rates 75
   6.4 Symbol Timing 75
   6.5 Latency Buffer 75

7. Station Attachment Specifications—Shielded Twisted Pair 77
   7.1 Scope 77
   7.2 Overview 77
   7.3 Coupling of the Station to the Ring 78
   7.4 Ring Access Control 78
       7.4.1 Current and Voltage Limits 78
       7.4.2 Insertion/Bypass Transfer Timing...................... 80
   7.5 Signal Characteristics 80
       7.5.1 Transmitted Signals 80
       7.5.2 Received Signals................................... 80
   7.6 Reliability 82
   7.7 Safety and Grounding Requirements 83
   7.8 Electromagnetic Susceptibility 83
   7.9 Medium Interface Connector (MIC) 83
       7.9.1 Medium Interface Connector—Contactor Detail 84
       7.9.2 Medium Interface Connector—Locking Mechanism Detail 84
   7.10 References 84

APPENDIX   PAGE

Hierarchical Structuring for Locally Administered Addresses 87
    A1. General Structure 87
    A2. Group Addressing Modes 88

FIGURES
Fig 2-1   Relation of OSI Reference Model to LAN Model   23
Fig 2-2   Token Ring Configuration   24
Fig 3-1   MAC Frame Information Field Structure   32
Fig 4-1   An Example of a Failure Domain   44
Fig 4-2   Receive Action Table   48
Fig 4-3   Operational Finite-State Machine Diagram   50
Fig 4-4   Bit Flipping Loop State Table   51
Fig 4-5   Standby Monitor Finite-State Machine Diagram   54
Fig 4-6   Active Monitor Finite-State Machine Diagram   58
Fig 6-1   Example of Symbol Encoding   74
Fig 7-1   Partitioning of the Physical Layer and Medium   77
Fig 7-2   Example of Station Connection to the Medium   79
Fig 7-3   Receive Filter Characteristics for 4 Mbit/s Operational
            150Ω Impedance   81
Fig 7-4   Receive Signal Eye Pattern   82
Fig 7-5   Medium Interface Connector—Isometric View   83
Fig 7-6   Medium Interface Connector—Contactor Detail   85
Fig 7-7   Medium Interface Connector—Locking Mechanism Detail   86

An American National Standard

IEEE Standards for
Local Area Networks:

Token Ring Access Method and
Physical Layer Specifications

1. General

1.1 Scope. For the purpose of compatible interconnection of data processing equipment via a local area network using the token-passing ring access method, this IEEE standard:

(1) Defines the frame format, including delimiters, addressing, and frame check sequence, and introduces medium access control frames, timers, and priority stacks (see Section 3);

(2) Defines the medium access control protocol. The finite-state machine and state tables are supplemented with a prose description of the algorithms (see Section 4);

(3) Describes the services provided by the medium access control sublayer to the network management and the logical link control sublayer and the services provided by the physical layer to network management and the medium access control sublayer. These services are defined in terms of service primitives and associated parameters (see Section 5);

(4) Defines the physical layer functions of symbol encoding and decoding, symbol timing, and latency buffering (see Section 6);

(5) Defines the 1 and 4 Mb/s, shielded twisted pair attachment of the station to the medium including the definition of the medium interface connector (see Section 7).

NOTE: The definition of suitable media (twisted pair, coaxial cable, and optical fiber) for connecting stations that meet the attachment standard specified herein is a subject for future consideration. Until such time as specific media are specified, the specifications in Section 7 shall define the performance bounds to which an operating network, including media and trunk coupling unit(s), shall conform.

A particular emphasis of this standard is to specify the homogeneous, externally visible characteristics needed for interconnection compatibility, while avoiding unnecessary constraints upon and changes to internal design and implementation of the heterogeneous processing equipment to be interconnected.

1.2 Definitions

abort sequence. A sequence that terminates the transmission of a frame prematurely.

broadcast transmission. A transmission addressed to all stations.

differential Manchester encoding. A signalling method used to encode clock and data bit information into bit symbols. Each bit symbol is split into two halves, where the second half is the inverse symbol of the first half. A 0 bit is represented by a polarity change at the start of the bit time. A 1 bit is represented by no polarity change at the start of the bit time. Differential Manchester encoding is polarity independent.

fill. A bit sequence that may be either 0 bits, 1 bits, or any combination thereof.

frame. A transmission unit that carries a protocol data unit (PDU) on the ring.

logical link control (LLC). That part of the data link layer that supports media independent data link functions, and uses the services of the medium access control sublayer to provide services to the network layer.

medium. The material on which the data may be represented. Twisted pairs, coaxial cables, and optical fibers are examples of media.

medium access control (MAC). The portion of the IEEE 802 data station that controls and mediates the access to the ring.

medium interface connector (MIC). The connector between the station and trunk coupling unit (TCU) at which all transmitted and received signals are specified.

monitor. The monitor is that function that recovers from various error situations. It is contained in each ring station; however, only the monitor in one of the stations on a ring is the *active monitor* at any point in time. The monitor function in all other stations on the ring is in standby mode.

multiple frame transmission. A transmission where more than one frame is transmitted when a token is captured.

network management (NMT). The conceptual control element of a station which interfaces with all of the layers of the station and is responsible for the setting and resetting of control parameters, obtaining reports of error conditions, and determining if the station should be connected to or disconnected from the medium.

physical (PHY) layer. The layer responsible for interfacing with the medium, detecting and generating signals on the medium, and converting and processing signals received from the medium and the medium access control layer.

protocol data unit (PDU). Information delivered as a unit between peer entities which contains control information and, optionally, data.

repeat. The action of a station in receiving a bit stream (for example, frame, token, or fill) from the previous station and placing it on the medium to the next station. The station repeating the bit stream may copy it into a buffer or modify control bits as appropriate.

repeater. A device used to extend the length, topology, or interconnectivity of the transmission medium beyond that imposed by a single transmission segment.

ring latency. In a token ring medium access control system, the time (measured in bit times at the data transmission rate) required for a signal to propagate once around the ring. The ring latency time includes the signal propagation delay through the ring medium plus the sum of the propagation delays through each station connected to the token ring.

service data unit (SDU). Information delivered as a unit between adjacent entities which may also contain a PDU of the upper layer.

station (or data station). A physical device that may be attached to a shared medium local area network for the purpose of transmitting and receiving information on that shared medium. A data station is identified by a destination address.

token. The symbol of authority that is passed between stations using a token access method to indicate which station is currently in control of the medium.

transmit. The action of a station generating a frame, token, abort sequence, or fill and placing it on the medium to the next station. In use, this term contrasts with repeat.

trunk cable. The transmission cable that interconnects two trunk coupling units.

trunk coupling unit (TCU). A physical device that enables a station to connect to a trunk cable. The trunk coupling unit contains the means for inserting the station into the ring or, conversely, bypassing the station.

2. General Description

This standard specifies the formats and protocols used by the token-passing ring medium access control (MAC) sublayer, the physical (PHY) layer, and the means of attachment to the token-passing ring physical medium. The Local Area Network (LAN) model and its relationship to the Open Systems Interconnection (OSI) Reference Model of the International Organization for Standardization (ISO) is illustrated in Fig 2-1.

A token ring consists of a set of stations serially connected by a transmission medium. (See Fig 2-2.) Information is transferred sequentially, bit by bit, from one active station to the next. Each station generally regenerates and repeats each bit and serves as the means for attaching one or more devices (terminals, work-stations) to the ring for the purpose of communicating with other devices on the network. A given station (the one that has access to the medium) transfers information onto the ring, where the information circulates from one station to the next. The addressed destination station(s) *copies* the information as it passes. Finally, the station that transmitted the information effectively removes the information from the ring.

Fig 2-1
Relation of OSI Reference Model to LAN Model

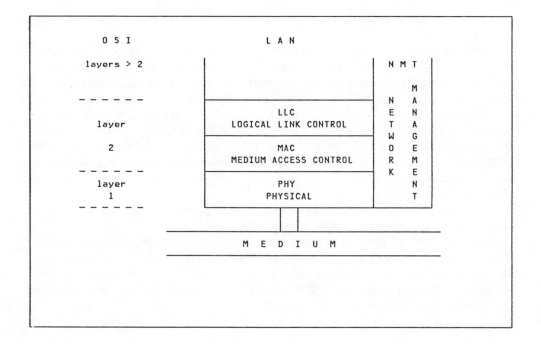

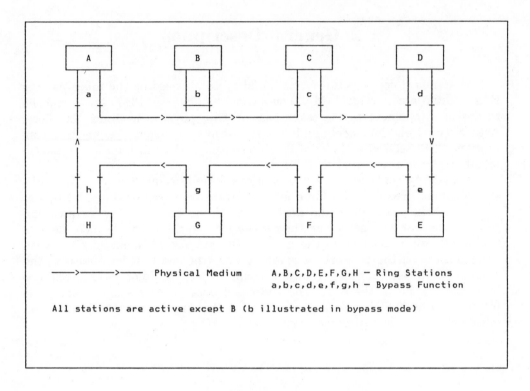

Fig 2-2
Token Ring Configuration

A station gains the right to transmit its information onto the medium when it detects a token passing on the medium. The token is a control signal comprised of a unique signalling sequence that circulates on the medium following each information transfer. Any station, upon detection of an appropriate token, may capture the token by modifying it to a start-of-frame sequence and appending appropriate control and status fields, address fields, information field, frame-check sequence and the end-of-frame sequence. At the completion of its information transfer and after appropriate checking for proper operation, the station initiates a new token, which provides other stations the opportunity to gain access to the ring.

A token holding timer controls the maximum period of time a station shall use (occupy) the medium before passing the token.

Multiple levels of priority are available for independent and dynamic assignment depending upon the relative class of service required for any given message, for example, synchronous (real-time voice), asynchronous (interactive), immediate (network recovery). The allocation of priorities shall be by mutual agreement among users of the network.

Error detection and recovery mechanisms are provided to restore network operation in the event that transmission errors or medium transients (for example, those resulting from station insertion or removal) cause the access method to deviate from normal operation. Detection and recovery for these cases utilize a network monitoring function that is performed in a specific station with back-up capability in all other stations that are attached to the ring.

3. Formats and Facilities

3.1 Formats. There are two basic formats used in token rings: tokens and frames. In the following discussion, the figures depict the formats of the fields *in the sequence they are transmitted on the medium*, with the left-most bit or symbol transmitted first.

Processes, which require comparison of fields or bits, perform that comparison upon those fields or bits *as depicted*, with the left-most bit or symbol compared first, and for the purpose of comparison, considered most significant.

3.1.1 Token Format

SD	AC	ED

SD = Starting Delimiter (1 octet)
AC = Access Control (1 octet)
ED = Ending Delimiter (1 octet)

The token shall be the means by which the right to transmit (as opposed to the normal process of repeating) is passed from one station to another.

3.1.2 Frame Format

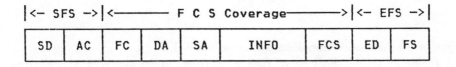

```
|<- SFS ->|<———————— F C S Coverage————————>|<- EFS ->|
| SD | AC | FC | DA | SA | INFO | FCS | ED | FS |
```

SFS = Start-of-Frame Sequence
SD = Starting Delimiter (1 octet)
AC = Access Control (1 octet)
FC = Frame Control (1 octet)
DA = Destination Address (2 or 6 octets)
SA = Source Address (2 or 6 octets)

INFO = Information (0 or more octets)*
FCS = Frame-Check Sequence (4 octets)
EFS = End-of-Frame Sequence
ED = Ending Delimiter (1 octet)
FS = Frame Status (1 octet)

---

* See 3.2.5 for limitation of information field length.

The frame format shall be used for transmitting both medium access control (MAC) and logical link control (LLC) messages to the destination station(s). It may or may not have an information (INFO) field.

3.1.2.1 Abort Sequence

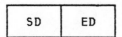

This sequence shall be used for the purpose of terminating the transmission of a frame prematurely. The abort sequence may occur anywhere in the bit stream; that is, receiving stations shall be able to detect an abort sequence even if it does not occur on octet boundaries.

3.1.3 Fill. When a station is transmitting (as opposed to repeating), it shall transmit fill preceding or following frames, tokens, or abort sequences to avoid what would otherwise be an inactive or indeterminate transmitter state.

Fill may be either 0 or 1 bits or any combination thereof and may be *any number* of bits in length, within the constraints of the token holding timer.

3.2 Field Descriptions. The following is a detailed description of the individual fields in the tokens and frames.

3.2.1 Starting Delimiter (SD)

J = non-data-J
K = non-data-K
0 = binary zero

(For a discussion of non-data symbols, see 6.1.)

A frame or token shall be started with these eight symbols. If otherwise, it shall not be considered valid.

3.2.2 Access Control (AC)

PPP = priority bits
T = token bit
M = monitor bit
RRR = reservation bits

3.2.2.1 Priority Bits. The priority bits shall indicate the priority of a token and, therefore, which stations are allowed to use the token. In a multiple-priority system, stations use different priorities depending on the priority of the PDU to be transmitted.

The eight levels of priority increase from the lowest (000) to the highest (111) priority. For purposes of comparing priority values, the priority shall be transmitted most significant bit first; for example, 110 has higher priority than 011 (left-most bit transmitted first).

3.2.2.2 Token Bit. The token bit is a 0 in a token and a 1 in a frame. When a station with a PDU to transmit detects a token which has a priority equal to or less than the PDU to be transmitted, it may change the token to a start-of-frame sequence and transmit the PDU.

3.2.2.3 Monitor Bit. The monitor bit is used to prevent a token whose priority is greater than 0 or any frame from continuously circulating on the ring. If an active monitor detects a frame or a high priority token with the monitor bit equal to 1, the frame or token is aborted.

This bit shall be transmitted as 0 in all frames and tokens. The active monitor inspects and modifies this bit. All other stations shall repeat this bit as received.

3.2.2.4 Reservation Bits. The reservation bits allow stations with high priority PDUs to request (in frames or tokens as they are repeated) that the next token be issued at the requested priority. The precise protocol for setting these bits is described in 4.2.2.

The eight levels of reservation increase from 000 to 111. For purposes of comparing reservation values, the reservation shall be transmitted most significant bit first; for example, 110 has higher priority than 011 (left-most bit transmitted first).

3.2.3 Frame Control (FC)

F F	Z Z Z Z Z Z

FF   = frame-type bits
ZZZZZZ = control bits

The FC field defines the type of the frame and certain MAC and information frame functions.

3.2.3.1 Frame-Type Bits. The frame-type bits shall indicate the type of the frame as follows:

00 = MAC frame (contains an MAC PDU)
01 = LLC frame (contains an LLC PDU)
1x = undefined format (reserved for future use)

Medium Access Control (MAC) Frames. If the frame-type bits indicate a MAC frame, all stations on the ring shall interpret and, based on the finite state of the station, act on the ZZZZZZ control bits.

Logical Link Control (LLC) Frames. If the frame-type bits indicate an LLC frame, the ZZZZZZ bits are designated as rrrYYY. The rrr bits are reserved and shall be transmitted as 0's in all transmitted frames and ignored upon reception. The YYY bits may be used to carry the priority (Pm) of the PDU from the source LLC entity to the target LLC entity or entities. Note that P (the priority in the access control [AC] field of a frame) is less than or equal to Pm when the frame is transmitted onto the ring.

Undefined Format. The value, 1x, is reserved for frame types that may be defined in the future. However, although currently undefined, any future frame formats shall adhere to the following conditions:

(1) The format shall be delimited by the 2-octet start-of-frame sequence (SFS) field and the 2-octet end-of-frame sequence (EFS) field, as defined in this standard. Additional fields may follow the EFS field.

(2) The position of the frame control (FC) field shall be unchanged.

(3) The SFS and EFS of the format shall be separated by an integral number of octets. This number shall be at least 1 (that is, the FC field) and the maximum length is subject to the constraints of the THT.

(4) All symbols between the SFS and EFS shall be 0 and 1 bits.

(5) All stations on the ring check for data symbols and an integral number of octets between the SFS and EFS fields. The error-detected bit of formats that are repeated shall be set to 1 when a non-data symbol or a non-integral number of octets is detected between the SFS and EFS fields.

(6) All bit errors that occur in the FC field that have a hamming distance of less than four must be detectable by stations using this format and shall not be accepted by any other station conforming to this standard.

3.2.4 Destination and Source Address (DA and SA) Fields. Each frame shall contain two address fields: the destination (station) address and the source (station) address, in that order. Addresses may be either 2 or 6 octets in length; however, all stations of a specific LAN shall have addresses of equal length.

3.2.4.1 Destination Address (DA). The destination address identifies the station(s) for which the information field of the frame is intended. Included in the destination address is a bit to indicate whether the destination address is an individual or group address and, for 48-bit addresses only, the second bit indicates whether it is a universally or locally administered address.

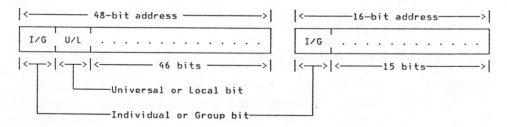

Individual and Group Addresses. The first bit transmitted of the destination address distinguishes individual from group addresses:

0 = individual address
1 = group address

Individual addresses identify a particular station on the LAN and shall be distinct from all other individual station addresses on the same LAN (in the case of local administration), or from the individual addresses of other LAN stations on a global basis (in the case of universal administration).

A group address shall be used to address a frame to multiple destination stations. Group addresses may be associated with zero or more stations on a given LAN.

NOTE: A group address is an address associated by convention with a group of logically related stations.

Broadcast Address. The group address consisting of 16 or 48 1's (for 2- or 6-octet addressing, respectively) shall constitute a broadcast address, denoting the set of all stations on a given LAN.

Null Address. An address of 16 or 48 0's (for 2- or 6-octet addressing, respectively) shall be considered a null address. It will mean the frame is not addressed to any particular station.

Address Administration. There are two methods of administering the set of 48-bit station addresses: locally or through a universal authority. The second bit transmitted of the destination address (DA) indicates whether the address has been assigned by a universal or local administrator:

0 = universally administered
1 = locally administered

Universal Administration. With this method, all individual addresses are distinct from the individual addresses of all other LAN stations on a global basis. The procedure for administration of these addresses is not specified in this standard.

Local Administration. Individual station addresses are administered by a local (to the LAN) authority. (This is the only method allowed for 16-bit addresses.)

NOTE: Appendix A contains a suggested method for hierarchical structuring of locally administered addresses.

3.2.4.2 Source Address (SA) Field. The source address shall identify the station originating the frame and shall have the same format and length as the DA in a given frame. The individual/group bit shall be 0.

3.2.5 Information (INFO) Field. The information field contains 0, 1, or more octets that are intended for MAC, NMT, or LLC. Although there is no maximum length specified for the information field, the time required to transmit a frame may be no greater than the token holding period that has been established for the station.

The format of the information field is indicated in the frame-type bits of the FC field. The frame types defined are MAC frame and LLC frame.

3.2.5.1 MAC Frame Format. Figure 3-1 defines the format of the information field, when present, for MAC frames.

Vector. The fundamental unit of MAC and NMT information. A vector contains its length, an identifier of its function, and zero or more subvectors. Only one vector is permitted per MAC frame.

VL (vector length). A 16-bit binary number that gives the length, in octets, of the vector. The length includes the VL field and can have values such that $X'0004' \leq VL \leq X'FFFF'$ (subject to the constraints of the token holding timer).

VI (vector identifier). A 2-octet code point that identifies the vector.

SV (subvector). Vectors require all data or modifiers to be contained within subvectors. One subvector is required to contain each piece of data or modifier that is being transported. A subvector is not position-dependent within a vector, but rather, each subvector must be identified by its subvector identifier.

SVL (subvector length). An 8-bit binary number that gives the length, in octets, of the subvector. The length includes the length of the SVL field. A subvector length of $X'FF'$ means that the subvector is longer than 254 octets and the actual length is included in the next two octets.

Fig 3-1
MAC Frame Information Field Structure

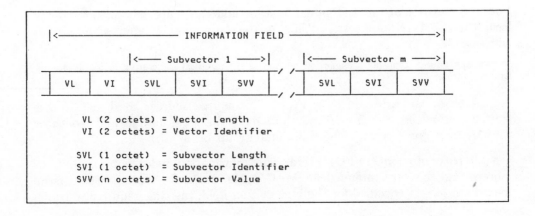

SVI (subvector identifier). A 1-octet code point that identifies the subvector. The code point of X'FF' indicates that an expanded identifier is being used and is contained in the next two octets.

The subvectors are of two types. The subvectors with code points from X'00' through X'7F' are used so that certain specific, common (to many vectors) strings of MAC or NMT data can be formatted and labeled in a standard manner. This standardization is intended to facilitate sharing of data between MAC and NMT applications and make the data as application-independent as possible.

The subvectors with code points from X'80' through X'FE' are for specific definition within a particular vector by vector identifier. For example, the subvector X'90' can have an entirely different definition in every different vector. The subvector X'40' has only one definition across all vectors and applications.

Subvectors themselves may contain other subvectors and other types of vectors and optional fields which are unique only to the particular subvector to which they belong.

3.2.5.2 LLC Frame Format. The format of the information field for LLC frames is not specified in this standard. However, in order to promote interworking among stations, all stations shall be capable of receiving frames whose information field is up to and including 133 octets in length. (See ANSI/IEEE Std 802.2-1985 for additional information.)

3.2.5.3 Order of Bit Transmission. Each octet of the information field shall be transmitted most significant bit first.

3.2.6 Frame-Check Sequence (FCS). The FCS shall be a 32-bit sequence based on the following standard generator polynomial of degree 32.

$$G(X) = X^{32} + X^{26} + X^{23} + X^{22} + X^{16} + X^{12} + X^{11} + X^{10} + X^8 + X^7 + X^5 + X^4 + X^2 + X + 1$$

The FCS shall be the 1's complement of the sum (modulo 2) of the following:

(1) The remainder of $X^{**}k \cdot (X^{31} + X^{30} + X^{29} + \ldots + X^2 + X + 1)$ divided (modulo 2) by G(X), where k is the number of bits in the FC, DA, SA, and INFO fields;

(2) The remainder after multiplication by X^{32} and then division (modulo 2) by G(X) of the content (treated as a polynomial) of the FC, DA, SA, and INFO fields.

The FCS shall be transmitted commencing with the coefficient of the highest term.

As a typical implementation, at the transmitter, the initial remainder of the division is preset to all 1's and is then modified by division of the FC, DA, SA, and INFO fields by the generator polynomial, G(X). The 1's complement of this remainder is transmitted, most significant bit (MSB) first, as the FCS.

At the receiver, the initial remainder is preset to all 1's and the serial incoming bits of FC, DA, SA, INFO, and FCS, when divided by G(X), results in the absence of transmission errors, in a unique non-zero remainder value. The unique remainder value is the polynomial:

$$X^{31} + X^{30} + X^{26} + X^{25} + X^{24} + X^{18} + X^{15} + X^{14} + X^{12} + X^{11} + X^{10} + X^8 + X^6 + X^5 + X^4 + X^3 + X + 1$$

3.2.7 Ending Delimiter (ED)

J = non-data-J
K = non-data-K
1 = binary one
I = intermediate frame bit
E = error-detected bit

The transmitting station shall transmit the delimiter as shown. Receiving stations shall consider the ending delimiter (ED) valid if the first six symbols J K 1 J K 1 are received correctly.

3.2.7.1 Intermediate Frame Bit (I Bit). To indicate that this is an intermediate (or first) frame of a multiple frame transmission, the I bit shall be transmitted as 1. An I bit of 0 indicates the last or only frame of the transmission.

3.2.7.2 Error-Detected Bit (E Bit). The error-detected bit (E) shall be transmitted as 0 by the station that originates the token, abort sequence, or frame. All stations on the ring check tokens and frames for errors (for example, FCS error, non-data symbols: see 4.2.1). The E bit of tokens and frames that are repeated shall be set to 1 when a frame with error is detected; otherwise the E bit is repeated as received.

3.2.8 Frame Status (FS).

A = address-recognized bits
C = frame-copied bits
r = reserved bits

reserved bits. These bits are reserved for future standardization. They shall be transmitted as 0's; however, their value shall be ignored by the receivers.

3.2.8.1 Address-Recognized (A) Bits and Frame-Copied (C) Bits. The A and C bits shall be transmitted as 0 by the station originating the frame. If another station recognizes the destination address as its own address or relevant group address, it shall set the A bits to 1. If it copies the frame (into its receive buffer), it shall also set the C bits to 1. This allows the originating station to differentiate among three conditions:

(1) Station non-existent/non-active on this ring
(2) Station exists but frame not copied
(3) Frame copied

The A and C bits shall be set without regard to the value of the E bit and only if the frame is *good* as defined in 4.2.1. Only the values that are 00rr 00rr, 10rr 10rr, and 11rr 11rr shall be considered valid. All other values are invalid and ignored by the receiver.

NOTE: If a destination station detects that the A bits have already been set, and the DA is not a group address, it may imply a duplicate address problem exists. The second condition (station existent but frame not copied) allows the originating station to log the instances when, for example, congestion has prevented a destination station from copying the frame.

3.3 MAC Frames. The following are descriptions of various MAC frames that are used in the management of the token ring. Values for PDU priority (Pm), FC, DA, and INFO field content (Vector Identifier—VI, Subvector Identifier—SVI, and Subvector Value—SVV) associated with the particular MAC Supervisory Frame, are indicated.

Frames with the following FC values are to be handled as listed:

(1) If the value of the FC of the frame is X'00' and it is addressed to the station, it will be copied only if there is sufficient free buffer available for copying.

(2) If the value of the FC of the frame is X'01' and it is addressed to the station, every effort will be made to copy the frame including overwriting previously received information.

(3) If the value of the FC of the frame is greater than X'01', it will be addressed to all stations on the ring. It will be copied only if there is sufficient free buffer available for copying. If the frame is not copied, action will be based on the value of the FC field.

The digits enclosed by X' and ' (for example, X'07'), are the hexadecimal value of the assigned code point. Values, other than those defined below, will be ignored by the receiving station(s). All unassigned values are reserved for future specification. The general format for the information field of MAC frames is described under 3.2.5.

3.3.1 Claim Token MAC Frame (CL_TK). When a station that is in standby state determines that there is no active monitor operating on the ring, it shall enter a *claiming token* state. While in this state the station shall send claim token frames and inspect the source address of the claim token MAC frames it receives. If the SA matches its own (MA) address and subvector 1 matches the SUA, it has claimed the token and shall enter active monitor mode and generate a new token. (For a more detailed description, see Fig 4-5, the Standby Monitor Finite-State Machine Diagram.)

The CL_TK values are as follows:
Pm: Zero
FC: 00 000011   (Claim Token)
DA: All stations, this ring
VI: X'0003'   (Claim Token)
SVI-1: X'02'   (RUA—Received Upstream Neighbor's Address)
SVV-1: ———   (2- or 6-octet address)

3.3.2 Duplicate Address Test MAC Frame (DAT). This frame is transmitted with DA = MA as part of the initialization process. If the frame returns with the A bits set to 1, it indicates that there is another station on the ring with the same address. If such an event occurs, the station's network manager is notified and the station returns to bypass state. A station that copies a DAT frame will ignore it.

The DAT values are as follows:

Pm: Zero
FC: 00 000000
DA: MA   (This station's address)
VI: X'0007'   (Duplicate Address Test)

3.3.3 Active Monitor Present MAC Frame (AMP). This frame is transmitted by the active monitor. It shall be queued for transmission following the successful purging of the ring or following the expiration of the TAM. Any station in standby state that receives this frame shall reset its TSM.

The AMP values are as follows:

Pm: Pr*
FC: 00 000101
DA: All stations, this ring
VI: X'0005'   (Active Monitor Present)
SVI-1: X'02'   (RUA—Received Upstream Neighbor's Address)
SVV-1: ———   (2- or 6-octet address)

---

*An AMP is transmitted at the ring service priority (Pr) that exists at the time a token is received after an AMP PDU is queued. The default value for Pm for this frame is seven; see 5.3.2.1 to change this value.

3.3.4 Standby Monitor Present MAC Frame (SMP). This frame is transmitted by the standby monitor(s). After receipt of an AMP or SMP frame whose A and C bits equal 0, the TQP is reset. When timer TQP expires, an SMP PDU shall be queued for transmission.

The queuing of a SMP PDU is delayed for a period of TQP to assure that the transmission of SMP frames do not use more than 1% of the bandwidth of the ring in any TQP period of time.

The SMP values are as follows:

Pm:	Zero	
FC:	00 000110	
DA:	All stations, this ring	
VI:	X'0006'	(Standby Monitor Present)
SVI-1:	X'02'	(RUA—Received Upstream Neighbor's Address)
SVV-1:	——————	(2- or 6-octet address)

NOTE: Stations that receive an AMP or SMP frame in which the value of the A and C bits are 0 will regard the frame as having originated from their upstream neighbor's station. Therefore, a station that copies such a frame shall record the source address contained in the frame as the SUA for later transmission as a subvector in certain MAC frames as well as performing a comparison with certain MAC frames.

3.3.5 Beacon MAC Frame (BCN). This frame shall be sent as a result of serious ring failure (for example, broken cable, jabbering station, etc). It is useful in localizing the fault. The transmission of beacon is covered in the Standby Monitor Finite-State Machine (Fig 8).

The immediate upstream station is part of the failure domain about which the beacon is reporting. Therefore, as noted above, the address of the upstream station that was previously recorded is included in the MAC INFO field.

The BCN values are as follows:

Pm:	Zero	
FC:	00 000010	
DA:	All stations, this ring	
VI:	X'0002'	(Beacon)
SVI-1:	X'02'	(RUA—Received Upstream Neighbor's Address)
SVV-1:	——————	(2- or 6-octet address)
SVI-2:	X'01'	(Beacon Type)
SVV-2:		

X'0001'—Issued by station during reconfiguration (for future study)
X'0002'—Continuous J symbols received
X'0003'—Timer TNT expired during claiming token; no FR_CL_TK received
X'0004'—Timer TNT expired during claiming token; FR_CL_TK (SA<MA) received

3.3.6 Purge MAC Frame (PRG). This frame is transmitted by the active monitor. It shall be transmitted following claiming the token or to perform reinitialization of the ring following the detection of an M bit set to 1 or the expiration of timer TVX.

The PRG values are as follows:

Pm:	Zero	
FC:	00 000100	
DA:	All stations, this ring	
VI:	X'0004'	(Purge)
SVI-1:	X'02'	(RUA—Received Upstream Neighbor's Address)
SVV-1:	———	(2- or 6-octet address)

3.4 Timers. The value of these timers shall be established by mutual agreement among the users of the LAN.

NOTE: The term *reset,* when applied to timers, is to be understood to mean the timer is *reset* to its initial value and (re)started.

3.4.1 Timer, Return to Repeat (TRR). Each station shall have a timer TRR to ensure that the station shall return to Repeat State. TRR shall have a value greater than the maximum ring latency. The maximum ring latency consists of the signal propagation delay around a maximum-length ring plus the sum of all station latencies. The operation of TRR is described in the operational finite-state machine. The default time-out value of TRR shall be 2.5 ms.

3.4.2 Timer, Holding Token (THT). Each station shall have a timer THT to control the maximum period of time the station may transmit frames after capturing a token. A station may initiate transmission of a frame if such transmission can be completed before timer THT expires. The operation of THT is described in the operational finite-state machine. The default time-out value of THT shall be 10 ms.

3.4.3 Timer, Queue PDU (TQP). Each station shall have a timer TQP for the purpose of timing the enqueuing of an SMP PDU after reception of an AMP or SMP frame in which the A and C bits were equal to 0. The default time-out value of TQP is 10 ms.

3.4.4 Timer, Valid Transmission (TVX). Each station shall have a timer TVX which is used by the active monitor to detect the absence of valid transmissions. The operation of TVX is described in the monitor finite-state machine. The time-out value of TVX shall be the sum of the time-out value of THT plus the time-out value of TRR.

3.4.5 Timer, No Token (TNT). Each station shall have a timer TNT to recover from various token-related error situations. TNT shall have a time-out value equal to TRR plus n times THT (where n is the maximum number of stations on the ring). The operation of TNT is described in the monitor finite-state machines. The default time-out value of TNT shall be 1 s.

3.4.6 Timer, Active Monitor (TAM). Each station shall have a timer TAM which is used by the active monitor to stimulate the enqueuing of an AMP PDU for transmission. The default time-out value of timer TAM shall be 3 s.

3.4.7 Timer, Standby Monitor (TSM). Each station shall have a timer TSM which is used by the stand-by monitor(s) to assure that there is an active monitor on the ring and to detect a continuous stream of tokens. The default time-out value of timer TSM shall be 7 s.

3.5 Flags. Flags are used to *remember* the occurrence of a particular event. They shall be set when the event occurs. The flags used are:

I Flag: A flag which is set upon receiving an ED with the I bit equal to 0.

SFS Flag: A flag which is set upon receiving an SFS sequence.

MA Flag: A flag which is set upon receiving an SA which is equal to the station's address.

3.6 Priority Registers and Stacks.

Pr and Rr Registers: The value of the priority (P) and reservation (R) of the most recently received AC field are stored in registers as Pr and Rr.

Sr and Sx Stacks: If at the time of transmission of a token the value of Rr or Pm (the priority of a queued PDU) is greater than Pr, a token with a priority of the higher of Rr or Pm shall be transmitted. At the same time the station shall store the value of Pr in a stack as Sr and shall store the value of the priority of the token that was transmitted in a stack as Sx.

The use of the Pr and Rr registers and the Sr and Sx stacks in performing the priority function is described in detail in Section 4.

3.7 Latency Buffer. The latency buffer serves two purposes. The first is to ensure that there are at least 24 bits of latency in the ring. The second is to provide phase jitter compensation. The latency buffer is described in more detail in Section 6.

NOTE: The token management is structured so that only one latency buffer shall be active in a normally functioning ring and is provided by the active monitor in the ring.

4. Token Ring Protocols

This section specifies the procedures that shall be used in the medium access control (MAC) sublayer.

4.1 Overview. The subsections of 4.1 provide a descriptive overview of frame transmission and reception. The formal specification of the operation is given in 4.2.

4.1.1 Frame Transmission. Access to the physical medium (the ring) is controlled by passing a token around the ring. The token gives the downstream (receiving) station (relative to the station passing the token) the opportunity to transmit a frame or a sequence of frames. Upon request for transmission of an LLC PDU or NMT PDU, MAC prefixes the PDU with the appropriate FC, DA, and SA fields and enqueues it to await the reception of a token that may be used for transmission.

Such a token has a priority less than or equal to the priority of the PDU(s) that is to be sent. Upon queuing the PDU for transmission and prior to receiving a usable token, if a frame or an unusable token is repeated on the ring, the station requests a token of appropriate priority in the RRR bits of the repeated AC field. Upon receipt of a usable token, it is changed to a start-of-frame sequence by setting the token bit.

At this time, the station stops repeating the incoming signal and begins transmitting a frame. During transmission, the FCS for the frame is accumulated and appended to the end of the information field.

4.1.2 Token Transmission. After transmission of the frame(s) has been completed, the station checks to see if the station's address has returned in the SA field, as indicated by the MA_FLAG. If it has not been seen, the station transmits fill until the MA_FLAG is set, at which time the station transmits a token.

4.1.3 Stripping. After transmission of the token, the station will remain in transmit state until all of the frames that the station originated are removed from the ring. This is done to avoid unnecessary recovery action that would be caused if a frame were allowed to continuously circulate on the ring.

4.1.4 Frame Reception. Stations, while repeating the incoming signal stream, check it for frames they should copy or act upon. If the frame-type bits indicate a MAC frame, the control bits are interpreted by all stations on the ring. In addition, if the frame's DA field matches the station's individual address, relevant group address, or broadcast address, the FC, DA, SA, INFO, and FS fields are copied into a receive buffer and subsequently forwarded to the appropriate sublayer.

4.1.5 Priority Operation. The priority bits (PPP) and the reservation bits (RRR) contained in the access control (AC) field work together in an attempt to match the service priority of the ring to the highest priority PDU that is ready for transmission on the ring. As previously noted in 3.6, these values are stored in registers as Pr and Rr. The current ring service priority is indicated by the priority bits in the AC field, which is circulated on the ring.

The priority mechanism operates in such a way that *fairness* (equal access to the ring) is maintained for all stations within a priority level. This is accomplished by having the same station that raised the service priority level of the ring (the *stacking station)* return the ring to the original service priority. As previously noted in 3.6, the Sx and Sr stacks are used to perform this function.

The priority operation is explained as follows: When a station has a priority (a value greater than zero) PDU (or PDU's) ready to transmit, it requests a priority token. This is done by changing the reservation bits (RRR) as the station repeats the AC field. If the priority level (Pm) of the PDU that is ready for transmission is greater than the RRR bits, the station increases the value of RRR field to the value Pm. If the value of the RRR bits is equal to or greater than Pm, the reservation bits (RRR) are repeated unchanged.

After a station has claimed the token, the station transmits PDUs that are at or above the present ring service priority level until it has completed transmission of those PDUs or until the transmission of another frame could not be completed before timer THT expires (see 3.4.2). The priority of all of the PDUs that are transmitted should be at the present ring service priority value. The station will then generate a new token for transmission on the ring.

If the station does not have additional PDUs to transmit that have a priority (Pm) or does not have a reservation request (as contained in register Rr) neither of which is greater than the present ring service priority (as contained in register Pr), the token is transmitted with its priority at the present ring service priority and the reservation bits (RRR) at the greater of Rr or Pm and no further action taken.

However, if the station has a PDU ready for transmission or a reservation request (Rr), either of which is greater than the present ring service priority, the token is generated with its priority at the greater of Pm or Rr and its reservation bits (RRR) as 0. Since the station has raised the service priority level of the ring, the station becomes a stacking station and, as such, stores the value of the old ring service priority as Sr and the new ring service priority as Sx. (These values will be used later to lower the service priority of the ring when there are no PDU's ready to transmit on the ring whose Pm is equal to or greater than the stacked Sx.)

NOTE: Since a station may have raised the service priority of the ring more than once before the service priority is returned to a lower priority (for example, from 1 to 3 and then 5 to 6), it may have multiple Sx and Sr values stored and, hence, the term *stacked*. Also note that the terms *stack* and *stacked* are not to be confused with other usages of these same terms.

Having become a stacking station, the station claims every token that it receives that has a priority (PPP) equal to its highest stacked transmitted priority (Sx) in order to examine the RRR bits of the AC field for the purpose of raising, maintaining, or lowering the service priority of the ring. The new token is transmitted with its PPP bits equal to the value of the reservation bits (RRR) but no lower than the value of the highest stacked received priority (Sr), which was the original ring priority service level.

If the value of the new ring service priority (PPP equal to Rr) is greater than Sr, the RRR bits are transmitted as 0, the old ring service priority contained in Sx is replaced with a new value Sx equal to Rr, and the station continues its role as a stacking station.

However, if the Rr value is equal to or less than the value of the highest stacked received priority (Sr) the new token is transmitted at a priority value of the Sr, both Sx and Sr are removed *(popped)* from the stack, and if no other values of Sx and Sr are stacked, the station discontinues its role as a stacking station.

NOTE: A stacking station that has claimed the token may transmit PDUs as well as examining RRR bits, as described above. Of course only those PDUs which have a priority equal to or greater than the ring service priority may be transmitted.

The frames that are transmitted to initialize the ring have a PPP field that is equal to 0. The receipt of a PPP field whose value is less than a stacked Sx will cause any Sx or Sr values that may be stacked to be cleared in all stations on the ring.

The complete description of priority operating is contained in the Operational Finite-State Machine (see Fig 4-3).

4.1.6 Beaconing and Neighbor Notification. When a hard failure is detected in a token ring, its cause must be isolated to the proper failure domain so that recovery actions can take place. The failure domain consists of

(1) the station reporting the failure (the beaconing station)

(2) the station upstream of the beaconing station

(3) the ring medium between them

For example, if a failure occurred within the domain shown in Fig 4-1, station G would report upon it by transmitting beacon MAC frames.

A failure that causes bit disruption within the transmitter side of station F, in the medium between stations F and G, or within the receiver side of station G, will be detected and reported upon by station G using a beacon MAC frame. This alerts all other stations on the ring that the token protocol has been suspended until such a time that the disruption terminates or is removed.

To do accurate problem determination, all elements of the failure domain must be known at the time that the failure is detected. This implies that at any given time, each station should know the identity of its upstream neigh-

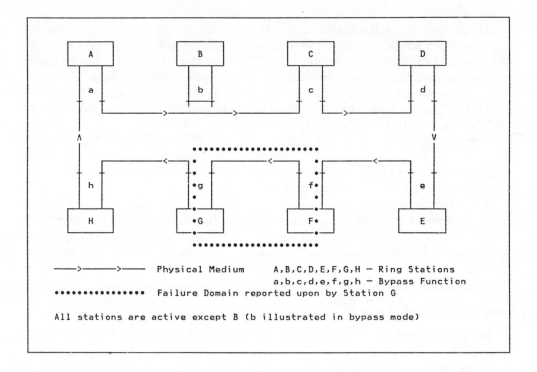

Fig 4-1
An Example of a Failure Domain

bor station. A process for obtaining this identity, known as Neighbor Notification, is described below.

Neighbor Notification has its basis in the address-recognized and frame-copied bits (the A and C bits) of the FS field. These bits are transmitted as 0's. If a station recognizes the destination address of the frame as one of its own, the station sets the A bits to 1 in the passing frame. If a station also copies the frame, then the C bits are also set to a 1.

When a frame is broadcast to all stations on a ring, the first station downstream of the broadcaster will see that the A and C bits are all 0's. Since a broadcast frame will have its destination address recognized by all of the stations on the ring, the first station downstream will, in particular, set the A bits to 1. All stations further downstream will, therefore, not see the A and C bits as all 0's. This process continues in a circular, daisy-chained fashion to let every station know the identity of its upstream neighbor (see the note under 3.3.4).

The monitor begins Neighbor Notification by broadcasting the active monitor present (AMP) MAC frame. The station immediately downstream from it takes the following actions:

(1) resets its timer TSM, based on seeing the AMP value in the FC field;

(2) if possible, copies the broadcast AMP MAC frame and stores the upstream station's identity in an upstream neighbor's address (UNA) memory location;

(3) sets the A bits (and C bits if the frame was copied) of the passing frame to 1's;

(4) at a suitable transmit opportunity, broadcasts a similar standby monitor present (SMP) MAC frame.

One by one, each station receives an SMP frame with the A and C bits set to 0's, stores its UNA, and continues the process by broadcasting such a frame itself.

Since the AMP frame must pass each station on a regular basis (the active monitor present MAC frame sent by the monitor), the continuous transmission of tokens onto a ring can be detected. In addition to the timer TAM in the active monitor, each standby station has a timer TSM that is reset each time an AMP MAC frame passes. If timer TSM expires, that standby monitor station begins transmitting claim token frames.

4.2 Specification. The operation of the ring is described in this section.

In the case of a discrepancy between the FSM diagrams/tables and the supporting text, the FSM diagrams/tables shall take precedence.

The MAC receives from the PHY layer a serial stream of symbols. Each symbol shall be one of the following:

$$0 = \text{binary zero}$$
$$1 = \text{binary one}$$
$$J = \text{non-data-J}$$
$$K = \text{non-data-K}$$

(See 6.1 for a detailed description of these symbols.)

From the received symbols MAC detects various types of input data, such as tokens, MAC frames, and LLC information frames.

In turn, MAC stores values, sets flags, and performs certain internal actions (as noted in Fig 4-2, Receive Action Table) as well as generating tokens, frames, or fill, or flipping bits and delivering them to the PHY layer in the form of a serial stream of the 0, 1, J, and K symbols.

For the purpose of accumulating the FCS and storing the contents of a frame, J and K symbols that are not part of the SD or ED shall be interpreted as 1 and 0 bits, respectively.

Finite-State Machine (FSM) Notation. The notation used in the FSM diagrams is as follows:

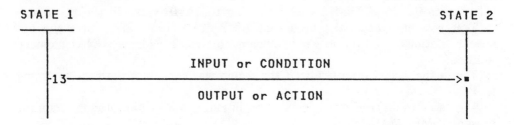

States are shown as vertical lines. Transitions are shown as horizontal lines with a number indicating the transition (for example, 13) and the arrow indicating the direction of transition.

The input or condition shown above the line is the requirement to make the transition. The output or action shown below the line occurs simultaneously with making the transition. The transition begins when the input occurs or the condition specified is met and is complete when the output or action has occurred. If the state transition is in progress, then no other FSM transition may be initiated.

If the exit conditions of a state are satisfied at the time the state is entered, no action is taken in that state and the state is immediately exited.

Abbreviations and Mnemonics (as used in FSM description)

A   = Address-Recognized Bit
AMP = Active Monitor Present
BCN   = Beacon
C   = Frame-Copied Bit
CL   = Claim
DA   = Destination Address
DAT = Duplicate Address Test
E   = Error Detected Bit
ED   = Ending Delimiter
EFS   = End-of-Frame Sequence
FR   = Frame
FS   = Frame Status (Field)
I   = Intermediate Frame Bit
M   = Monitor Bit
A   = My (station's) Address
MSI   = MA_STATUS.indication
NMT = Network Management
P   = Priority (of the AC)
PDU   = Protocol Data Unit
Pm   = PDU Priority
Pr   = Last Priority Value Received

PRG = Purge
R   = Reservation (of the AC)
RR = Last Reservation Value Received
RUA = Received Upstream Neighbor's Address
SUA = Stored Upstream Neighbor's Address
SA = Source Address
SFS = Start-of-Frame Sequence
SMP = Standby Monitor Present
Sr = Highest Stacked Received Priority
Sx = Highest Stacked Transmitted Priority
TAM = Timer, Active Monitor
THT = Timer, Holding Token
TK = Token
TNT = Timer, No Token
TQP = Timer, Queue PDU
TRR = Timer, Return to Repeat $\neg$ = Boolean NOT
TSM = Timer, Standby Monitor   & = AND
TVX = Timer, Valid Transmission   V = OR
TX = Transmit   / = the greater of

TK(P=x,M=y,R=z) = Token with P=x, M=y, and R=z
FR(P=x,M=y,R=z) = Frame with P=x, M=y, and R=z

4.2.1 Receive Actions. Three varieties of frame identification are used in the state transitions and at the service interfaces described in this standard: *good frame, validly formed frame*, and *frame with error*. These frame varieties are indicated by combinations of the following properties:

Properties of a Frame

(1) Is bounded by a valid SD and ED
(2) Has the E (error) bit equal to 0
(3) Is an integral number of octets in length
(4) Is composed of only 0 and 1 bits between the SD and ED
(5) Has the FF bits of the FC field equal to 00 or 01
(6) Has a valid FCS
(7) Has a minimum of 10 (2-octet addressing) or 18 (6-octet addressing) octets between SD and ED

The three frame varieties are defined below. This is not an inclusive list of all possible bit-sequence formats; for example, other format sequences known in this standard are the token and the abort sequence. Note that the value of the I, E, A, and C bits are not part of these definitions.

Good Frame (FR_GOOD). A bit sequence that satisfies the following condition, based on the properties of a frame listed above:

1 & 3 & 4 & 5 & 6 & 7

47

Validly Formed Frame. A bit sequence that satisfies the following condition:

1 & 3 & 5 & 7

Frame With Error (FR_WITH_ERROR). A bit sequence that satisfies the following condition:

1 & ($\neg$3 V $\neg$4 V (5&$\neg$6) V (5&$\neg$7))

The various internal actions that are taken as a result of an input received from the ring are summarized in the Receive Action Table (Fig 4-2). They are explained as follows:

(R-A) Report Frame Condition. The reporting actions for received frames are dependent upon the properties of a frame. Whenever one of the following report conditions is satisfied, MA_STATUS is indicated to NMT:

   (1) 1 & 2 & 3 & 4 & 5 & 6 & 7
   (2) 1 & $\neg$2 & 3 & 4 & 5 & 6 & 7
   (3) 1 & 2 & ($\neg$3 V $\neg$4 V (5 & $\neg$6) V (5 & $\neg$7))

(R-B) Priority Level Error. If there is a highest stacked transmitted priority (Sx) stored and a token is received with a priority (P) less than the value of Sx, then an error has occurred. Therefore, the stacks shall be cleared.

(R-C) My Address Received. If the source address that is received is equal to the station's individual address, the MA flag shall be set. Note that the MA flag shall be set without regard to whether it is a good frame, a validly formed frame, or a frame with error.

(R-D) Access Control Field Received. Upon the receipt of an access control (AC) field in a token or a frame, the value of the priority bits shall be stored as Pr, the reservation bits shall be stored as Rr, and the previously stored Pr and Rr shall be discarded.

(R-E) I Bit Equal Zero Received. If an end-of-frame sequence with I=0 is received the I_FLAG shall be set.

Fig 4-2
Receive Action Table

REF	RECEIVE	ACTION
R-A	REPORT FRAME CONDITION	MSI
R-B	TK(P<Sx)	CLEAR STACKS
R-C	SA=MA	SET MA_FLAG
R-D	TOKEN V FRAME	STORE (Pr, Rr)
R-E	I=0	SET I_FLAG
R-F	SFS	SET SFS_FLAG
R-G	FR_(SA=MA,RUA≠SUA)	MSI

(R-F) Start-of-Frame Sequence Received. If a start-of-frame sequence is received the SFS_FLAG shall be set.

(R-G) SA = MA and RUA and SUA Not Equal. If a MAC frame is received in which the SA equals the station's address and it contains an RUA (that is, BCN, CL_TK, AMP, SMP, or PRG frame) not equal to the SUA, MA_STATUS is indicated to MNT.

4.2.2 Operational Finite-State Machine. The operational finite-state machine (see Figs 4-3 and 4-4) is explained as follows:

4.2.2.1 Resume (Operational FSM Activity). When the station is in monitor states of Bypass, Inserted, Transmit Claim Token, Transmit Beacon, Transmit Fill, or Transmit Purge (for example, not in Initialize, Standby, or Active states), activity of the Operational FSM is suspended. Upon reentry into Initialize, Standby, or Active Monitor states, activity of the operational FSM shall be resumed in Repeat state.

4.2.2.2 State 0: REPEAT (Repeat State). In Repeat state, the bits that are received are, in general, repeated on the line to the next station. Certain bits and fields in the repeated bit stream may be modified and certain actions taken without changing state. Transition shall be made to State 1: TX DATA_FR (Transmit Data Frame[s]) when there are one or more PDUs queued for transmission and the conditions for transmission are satisfied. Transition shall be made to State 4: TX ZEROS & MOD STACKS (Transmit Zeros and Modify Stacks) for the purpose of modifying the priority stacks.

(01) Usable Token Received. If a PDU is queued for transmission and a token is received whose priority (P) is equal to or less than the PDU priority (Pm), the station shall change the token to a start-of-frame sequence (by changing the token bit from 0 to 1) and transmit M and R as 0, initiate the transmission of the enqueued PDU, reset the THT and the MA flag, and make a transition to State 1.

(02) Bit Flipping Loop. A number of actions may be taken without changing state. These actions are shown in Fig 4-4 and are explained as follows:

(02A) Request Usable Token. If there is a PDU queued for transmission with priority Pm, the reservation (R) shall be set to Pm on frames in which the reservation is less than Pm, and on tokens in which the priority is greater than Pm and the reservation is less than Pm and the priority is not equal to the highest stacked transmitted priority.

(02B) Frame With Error. The E (error) bit shall be transmitted as 1 if a frame with error is detected. (See Reference R-B in 4.2.1.)

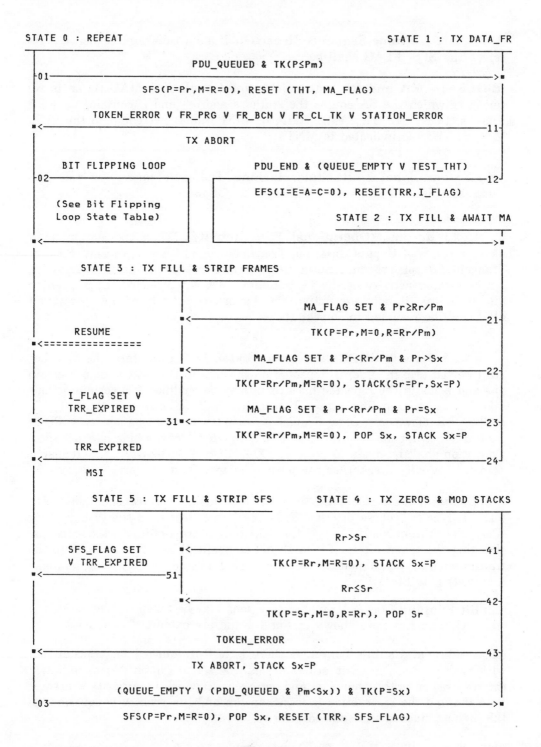

Fig 4-3
Operational Finite-State Machine Diagram

REF	INPUT	OUTPUT
02A	PDU_QUEUED &(FR(R<Pm) V TK(P>Pm>R,P≠Sx)	SET R=Pm
02B	FR_WITH_ERROR	SET E=1
02C	DA=MA (ADDRESS RECOGNIZED)	SET A=1
02D	FR_COPIED	SET C=1

Fig 4-4
Bit Flipping Loop State Table

(02C) Own Address Detected. If the station detected its own address or relevant group address in the DA field, the A bits in the FS field shall be transmitted as 1.

(02D) Frame Copied. If the station copies the frame from the ring, the C bits in the FS field shall be transmitted as 1.

(03) Re-stack Operation. If there are no frames enqueued with priority (Pm) equal to or greater than the highest stacked transmitted priority (Sx) and a token is received with priority (P) equal to the highest stacked transmitted priority (Sx), the following actions are taken. The token shall be changed to a start-of-frame sequence by changing the T bit from 0 to 1, popping the Sx from the stack, resetting timer TRR and the SFS flag, and making the transition to State 4. If there is no Sx value stacked, the test P=Sx shall be considered to be false.

4.2.2.3 State 1: TX DATA_FR (Transmit Data Frame[s]). While in this state, the station transmits one or more frames. The first and all subsequent PDU's that are transmitted shall have a Pm equal to or greater than the priority of the token that was used. All frames transmitted will have P equal to Pr and M and R equal to 0. On the receive side, as noted in Fig 4-2, the station shall monitor the receive data for the value of the priority and reservation bits, its station address, which has been transmitted in the source address field, and the ending delimiter.

(11) Abort State 1: Error Recovery Action. If after changing the token bit from a 0 to a 1, the station detects that the token did not end with an ED; or if a beacon, purge, or claim token frame is subsequently received; or if an error has occurred within the station, the transmission shall be terminated immediately with an abort sequence, the PDU dequeued, LLC notified of the event, and transition made to State 0.

(12) End-of-Frame Transmission. If the transmission of the PDU is completed (PDU_END) and there are no more PDU's to transmit at this priority or a higher priority (QUEUE_EMPTY), or if transmission of an additional frame could not be completed before THT expires (TEST_THT), an end-of-frame sequence (EFS) shall be transmitted with the I, E, A, and C bits equal to 0; timer TRR and the I flag shall be reset; and transition shall be made to State 2.

4.2.2.4 State 2: TX FILL & AWAIT MA (Transmit Fill and Await My Address). If a source address equal to the station's address has not been received (that is, MA_FLAG reset) the station shall transmit fill until MA_FLAG is set or TRR expires. If upon entering State 2, MA_FLAG is already set, transition shall be made directly to State 3 via transitions 21, 22, or 23.

(21) Token Transmission, Same Priority. If both the stored value Rr and a queued PDU priority (Pm) are less than or equal to the stored value Pr, a token shall be transmitted with the P equal to Pr, M equal to 0, and R equal to the greater of Rr or Pm, and transition shall be made to State 3.

(22) Token Transmission, Higher Priority, and Pr > Sx (Push Ring Priority). If the Rr or an enqueued PDU priority (Pm) is greater than the Pr, and the highest stacked transmitted priority (Sx) is less than the last priority value received (Pr), a token shall be transmitted with the P equal to the greater of Rr or Pm, and M and R equal to 0. Pr shall be stacked as Sr, P shall be stacked as Sx, and a transition made to State 3. If there is no Sx value stacked, the test Pr>Sx shall be considered true.

(23) Token Transmission, Higher Priority, and Pr = Sx (Pop Ring Priority). If the Rr or an enqueued PDU priority (Pm) is greater than the Pr, and the highest stacked transmitted priority (Sx) is equal to the last priority value received (Pr), a token shall be transmitted with the P equal to the greater of Rr or Pm, and M and R equal to 0. Sx shall be popped from the stack and a new value P shall be stacked as Sx and transition made to State 3. If there is no Sx value stacked, the test Pr=Sx shall be considered false.

(24) TRR Expires. If, while waiting for the MA flag to be set, timer TRR expires, transition shall be made directly to Repeat state (State 0) and MA_STATUS indicated to NMT.

4.2.2.5 State 3: TX FILL & STRIP FRAMES (Transmit Fill and Strip Frames). If an EFS with I equal to 0 has not been received (that is, I_FLAG reset) the station shall transmit fill until the I_FLAG is set or TRR expires. If upon entering State 3 the I_FLAG is already set or TRR has already expired, transition shall be made directly to State 0.

(31) Strip Complete. In this state, fill shall be transmitted until an EFS with I equal to 0 is received or TRR expires whereupon transition shall be made to State 0.

4.2.2.6 State 4: TX ZEROS & MOD STACK (Transmit Zeros and Modify Stack). A continuous string of 0's shall be transmitted immediately following the SFS until the internal logic of the station can perform the necessary functions to transmit a token.

Transmission of 0's may or may not terminate on an octet boundary. Note that this state shall cause consecutive SD's to exist on the ring without an intervening ED and that the SD of the transmitted token may not occur on an octet boundary relative to the transmitted 0's.

(41) Reservation Request (Rr) > Highest Stacked Received Priority (Sr). If Rr is greater than the highest stacked received priority Sr, a token with its priority (P) set to Rr and its M and R bits set to 0 shall be transmitted, P shall be stacked as Sx, and a transition shall be made to State 5.

(42) Reservation Request (Rr) ≤ Highest Stacked Received Priority (Sr). If Rr is equal to or less than the Sr, then a token with P equal to Sr, M equal to 0, and R equal to Rr shall be transmitted, Sr popped from the stack, and transition shall be made to State 5.

(43) Token Recognition Error. If after changing a token to a SFS, the station detects that the token did not end properly (with MRRR, JK1JK1), the transmission shall be terminated immediately with an abort sequence, Pr stacked as Sx, and transition shall be made to State 0.

4.2.2.7 State 5: TX FILL & STRIP SFS (Transmit Fill and Strip SFS). In this state, fill shall be transmitted until the transmitted SFS is received or TRR expires.

(51) Strip Complete. Upon receipt of the SFS or TRR expiring, transition shall be made to State 0.

4.2.3 Standby Monitor Finite-State Machine. (See Fig 4-5.) Upon coming on-line or after the station has been reset, (re)initialization is performed to assure that no other station on the ring has the same address as this station and that its (re)entry into the ring is known to its immediate downstream neighbor.

Upon completion of initialization, transition is made to Standby state where the ring is monitored to assure that there is a properly operating active monitor on the ring. It does so by observing the tokens and AMP frames as they are repeated on the ring. If tokens and AMP frames are not periodically detected, the standby monitor shall time-out and initiate claiming token.

The standby monitor utilizes timers TNT and TSM in its operation. When in Transmit Claim Token and Transmit Beacon states (States 3 and 5), the station shall utilize its own oscillator for transmission timing.

The standby monitor function is explained as follows:

4.2.3.1 Master Reset. If the station is reset, transition will be made from the current state of the monitor to Standby Monitor Bypass state (State 0). The latency buffer, if in use, will be deleted and all timers will be reset.

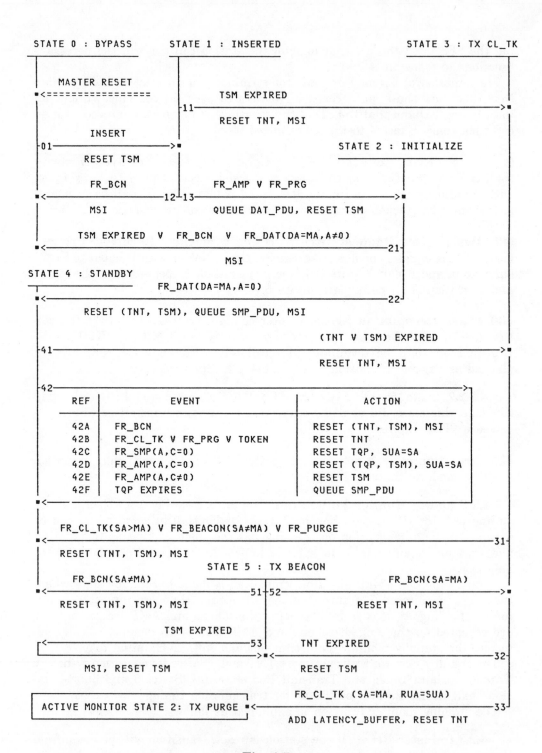

Fig 4-5
Standby Monitor Finite-State Machine Diagram

4.2.3.2 State 0: BYPASS. In this state the station is not inserted in the ring.

(01). Upon activation of the insertion logic (see 5.3.2.3), timer TSM is reset and transition made to State 1.

4.2.3.3 State 1: INSERTED. In this state the station synchronizes its receive clock with the receive signal and then, having achieved synchronization, repeats the received symbols on the line and awaits the receipt of an AMP or PRG.

(11). If an AMP or PRG is not received before timer TSM expires, it is assumed that there is no active monitor in the ring, timer TNT is reset, MA_STATUS is indicated, and transition is made to the Claiming Token state (State 3).

(12). If an FR_BCN is received, the station shall return to Bypass state (State 0) and the MA_STATUS shall be indicated.

(13). However, if AMP or PRG has been received, a Duplicate Address Test (DAT) PDU is enqueued for transmission awaiting the receipt of a usable token, timer TSM is reset, and transition made to Initialize state (State 2).

4.2.3.4 State 2: INITIALIZE. This state exists to detect the existence of a duplicate station address on the ring. This enhances the validity of later checks within the FSMs for SA=MA, etc. This is particularly useful in environments in which the station address assignments are not rigidly controlled. While in this state the station transmits the queued DAT_PDU when a usable token is received and repeats the received symbols on the line until one of the following events occur.

(21). If the DAT MAC frame that was transmitted by the station is not received before timer TSM has expired, or a beacon MAC frame is received, or a DAT MAC frame which the station originated (DA=MA) is received with the Address Recognized bits not set to 0, (A≠0) MA_STATUS is indicated to the NMT and the station returned to a Bypass state (State 0).

NOTE: NMT may determine if the station should retry insertion into the ring.

(22). However, if the DAT MAC frame is returned indicating that there is not another station on the ring with the same address (A=0), an SMP PDU is enqueued for transmission awaiting the receipt of a usable token, timers TNT and TSM are reset, MA_STATUS is indicated to NMT, and transition is made to Standby state (State 4).

4.2.3.5 State 3 : TX CLAIM_TOKEN (Transmit Claim Token). In this state, claim token MAC frames are continuously transmitted. If the SUA value is unknown, a null (all zeros) address will be used as the SUA.

(31). If a Claim Token MAC frame is received in which the source address is greater than the station's address, or a beacon frame is received in which the source address does not equal the station's address, or a purge frame is received, timers TNT and TSM are reset, MA_STATUS is indicated to NMT, and transition is made to Standby state (State 4).

(32). However, if timer TNT expires, timer TSM is reset, and transition is made to Beaconing state (State 5).

(33). Or, if the station receives a FR_CL_TK with a source address equal to the station's address and an RUA equal to the SUA, the bid for active monitor has been won. The latency buffer shall be inserted in the ring, timer TNT reset, and transition made to ACTIVE MONITOR Purge state (State 2).

4.2.3.6 State 4 : STANDBY. In this state the monitor is in standby mode, monitoring the ring to ascertain that there is a properly operating active monitor on the ring. It does so by observing the tokens and AMP frames as they are repeated on the ring. If tokens and AMP frames are not periodically detected, the standby monitor will time-out and initiate claiming token.

(41). If timers TNT or TSM expire, timer TNT is reset and transition made to Claiming Token state (State 3).

(42A). If a beacon frame is received, timers TNT and TSM are reset and MA_STATUS is indicated to NMT without changing state.

(42B). If a claim token frame, a purge frame, or a token is received, timer TNT is reset without changing state.

(42C). If an FR_SMP whose A and C bits equal 0 is received, the SA of the SMP frame shall be stored as the SUA, and timer TQP shall be reset.

(42D). If an FR_AMP whose A and C bits equal 0 is received, the SA of the AMP frame shall be stored as the SUA, and timers TQP and TSM shall be reset.

(42E). If an FR_AMP whose A and C bits do not equal 0 is received, timer TSM shall be reset.

(42F). If timer TQP expires, an SMP PDU shall be enqueued for transmission.

4.2.3.7 State 5 : TX BCN (Transmit Beacon). This state is entered when a serious ring failure has occurred. MAC supervisory beacon frames will continue to be transmitted until beacon MAC frames are received at which time:

(51). If SA does not equal MA, timers TNT and TSM shall be reset, MA_STATUS is indicated to NMT, and transition made to Standby state (State 4).

(52). However, if SA does equal MA then transition shall be made to Claiming Token state (State 3) after resetting timer TNT and indicating MA_STATUS.

(53). If, while transmitting FR_BCN, timer TSM expires, MA_STATUS will be indicated to NMT of the event and timer TSM reset.

4.2.4 Active Monitor Finite-State Machine. The function of the active monitor is to recover from various error situations such as absence of validly formed frames or tokens on the ring, a persistently circulating priority token, or a persistently circulating frame. In normal operation there is only one active monitor in a ring at any point in time. Timers TVX, TNT, TAM, and TRR are used by the active monitor.

The active monitor shall utilize its own oscillator to provide timing for all symbols repeated or transmitted on the ring. The active monitor also supplies the latency buffer for the ring.

The operation of the active monitor is explained in Fig 4-6.

4.2.4.1 State 0: ACTIVE. The active monitor is in this state when the ring is operating normally.

(01A). The M bit is set to 1 on a token whose M bit is 0 and whose priority is greater than 0 or a frame whose M bit is 0, and timer TVX reset.

(01B). Receipt of a token whose M bit and priority are 0 will cause timer TVX to be reset.

(01C). If timer TAM expires, an AMP PDU is enqueued for transmission awaiting the receipt of a usable token and timer TAM is reset without changing state.

(01D). If an FR_SMP whose A and C bits equal 0 is received, the SA of the SMP frame shall be stored as the SUA.

(02). If a frame or a token that is being repeated has its M bit equal to 1, the frame or token is aborted, timer TNT is reset, and transition made to Transmit Purge state (State 2).

(03). If timer TVX expires, timer TNT is reset, and transition made to Transmit Purge state (State 2).

(04). If the monitor station receives an AMP frame with a source address that does not equal the station's address, a purge frame, a claim token frame, or a beacon frame, the latency buffer shall be deleted, timers TNT and TSM reset, MA_STATUS indicated to NMT, and transition made to STANDBY MONITOR Standby state (State 4).

4.2.4.2 State 1: TX FILL (Transmit Fill). This state exists to assure that all purge frames have been stripped from the ring before transmitting a new token.

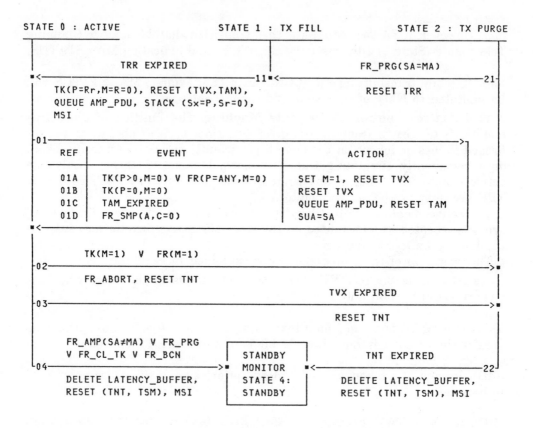

Fig 4-6
Active Monitor Finite-State Machine Diagram

(11). When timer TRR expires, a token is transmitted with P equal to Rr, and M and R equal to 0. P is stacked as Sx and a zero is stacked as Sr, timers TVX and TAM are reset, MA_STATUS indicated to NMT, and transition made to State 0.

4.2.4.3 State 2: TX PURGE (Transmit Purge). In this state, purge MAC frames are continuously transmitted to purge the ring before transmitting a new token.

(21). If the station receives an FR_PRG whose source address equals the station's address and, with a subvector equal to UNA, timer TRR is reset and transition is made to Transmit Fill state (State 1).

(22). If timer TNT expires while waiting for receipt of the station's source address, the latency buffer shall be deleted, timers TNT and TSM reset, MA_STATUS indicated to NMT, and transition made to STANDBY MONITOR Standby state (State 4).

5. Service Specifications

This section specifies the services provided:
(1) By the MAC sublayer to the Logical Link Control (LLC) sublayer
(2) By the PHY layer to the MAC sublayer
(3) By the MAC sublayer to NMT
(4) By the PHY layer to NMT
The services are described in an abstract way and do not imply any particular implementation or any exposed interface.

The diagram below serves as a guide to the subsections (5.1 through 5.4) that define the services provided.

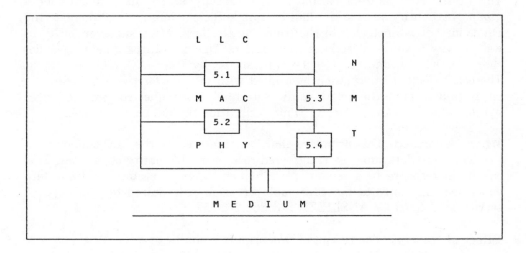

5.1 MAC to LLC Service. This section specifies the services required of the MAC sublayer by the LLC to allow the local LLC sublayer entity to exchange LLC data units with peer LLC sublayer entities.

5.1.1 Interactions. The following primitives are defined for the LLC sublayer to request service from the MAC sublayer:
MA_DATA.request
MA_DATA.indication
MA_DATA.confirmation
All primitives described in this section are mandatory.

5.1.2 Detailed Service Specifications. All primitives are specified in an exemplary form only. Each service shall name the particular primitive and the required information that is passed between the LLC sublayer and MAC sublayer.

5.1.2.1 MA__DATA.request. This primitive defines the transfer of a MAC service data unit from a local LLC sublayer entity to a single-peer LLC entity, or multiple-peer LLC entities in the case of group addresses.

Semantics of the Service Primitive

MA__DATA.request (

> frame__control,
> destination__address,
> m__sdu,
> requested__service__class
>)

The frame__control parameter specifies the value for the frame's FC octet. The destination__address parameter may specify either an individual or a group MAC entity address. It shall contain sufficient information to create the DA field that is appended to the frame by the local MAC sublayer entity as well as any lower-level address information. The m__sdu parameter specifies the MAC service data unit to be transmitted by the MAC sublayer entity. There is sufficient information associated with m__sdu for the MAC sublayer entity to determine the length of the data unit. The requested__service__class parameter specifies the priority (Pm) desired for the data unit transfer.

When Generated. This primitive shall be generated by the LLC sublayer entity whenever data must be transferred to a peer LLC entity or entities. This can be in response to a request from higher layers of protocol or from data generated internally to the LLC sublayer, such as required by LLC Type 2 service as defined by ANSI/IEEE Std 802.2-1985.

Effect of Receipt. The receipt of this primitive shall cause the MAC entity to append all MAC specific fields, including DA, SA, and any fields that are unique to the particular medium access method, and pass the properly formed frame to the lower layers of protocol for transfer to the peer MAC sublayer entity or entities.

Additional Comments. Requested__service__class is one of 8 levels.

5.1.2.2 MA__DATA.indication. This primitive defines the transfer of data from the MAC sublayer entity to the LLC sublayer entity or entities in the case of group addresses.

Semantics of the Service Primitive

MA__DATA.indication (

> frame__control,
> destination__address,
> source__address,
> m__sdu,
> reception__status
>)

The frame__control parameter is the FC octet received. The destination__address parameter may be either an individual or a group address as specified by the DA field of the incoming frame. The source__address parameter must be an individual address as specified by the SA field of the incoming frame. The m__sdu parameter shall specify the MAC service data unit as received by the local MAC entity. The reception__status parameter indicates the success or failure of the incoming frame. It consists of the following elements:

(1) frame__status: FR__GOOD, FR__WITH__ERROR. If an FR__WITH__ERROR is reported, the reason for the error shall also be reported. The reason shall be one of the following:

(a) invalid__FCS: calculated FCS does not match the received FCS

(b) code__violation: J or K symbol received between the SD and ED

(c) frame__truncated: the received frame, although free from errors, exceeded the internal buffer space

(d) short__frame: the received frame was shorter than the minimum

(2) E__value: zero, one, invalid

(3) A__&__C__value: zero__zero, one__zero, one__one, invalid

When Generated. The MA__DATA.indication primitive shall be generated by the MAC sublayer entity to the LLC sublayer entity or entities to indicate the arrival of an LLC frame at the local MAC sublayer entity. Such frames shall be reported only if they are validly formed and their destination address designates the local MAC entity, or the source address designates the local MAC entity if the station was so initialized (see 5.3.2.1).

Effect of Receipt. The effect of receipt of this primitive by the LLC sublayer is dependent upon the validity and content of the frame.

Additional Comments. If the local MAC sublayer entity is designated by the destination__address parameter of an MA__DATA.request primitive, the indication primitive shall also be invoked by the MAC entity to the local LLC entity. This full duplex characteristic of the MAC sublayer may be due to unique function capabilities within the MAC sublayer or full duplex characteristics of the lower layers; for example, all frames transmitted to the broadcast address shall invoke MA__DATA.indication primitives at all stations in the network including the station that generated the request.

5.1.2.3 MA__DATA.confirmation. This primitive has local significance and shall provide an appropriate response to the LLC sublayer MA__DATA.request primitive signifying the success or failure of the request.

Semantics of the Service Primitive

    MA__DATA.confirmation (
                              transmission__status,
                              provided__service__class
)

The transmission_status parameter shall be used to pass status information back to the local requesting LLC sublayer entity. It shall be used to indicate the success or failure of the previous associated MA_DATA.request. The provided_service_class parameter specifies the service class that was provided for the data unit transfer.

When Generated. This primitive shall be generated by the MAC entity in response to an MA_DATA.request primitive from the local LLC sublayer entity.

Effect of Receipt. The effect of receipt of this primitive by the LLC sublayer is unspecified.

Additional Comments. It is assumed that sufficient information is available to the LLC sublayer to associate the response with the appropriate request.

5.2 PHY to MAC Service. The services provided by the PHY layer allow the local MAC sublayer entity to exchange MAC data units with peer MAC sublayer entities.

NOTE. All PHY data units have the duration of one symbol period.

5.2.1 Interactions. The following primitives are defined for the MAC sublayer to request service from the PHY layer:
   PH_DATA.request
   PH_DATA.indication
   PH_DATA.confirmation
All primitives described in this section are mandatory.

5.2.2 Detailed Service Specifications. All primitives are specified in an exemplary form only. Each service shall name the particular primitive and the required information that shall be passed between the MAC sublayer and PHY layer.

5.2.2.1 PH_DATA.request. This primitive defines the transfer of data from a local MAC sublayer entity to the station's PHY layer.

Semantics of the Service Primitive

   PH_DATA.request (
                    symbol
)
The symbol specified shall be one of the following:
   0 = binary zero
   1 = binary one
   J = non-data-J
   K = non-data-K

When Generated. The MAC sublayer shall send the PHY layer a PH__DATA.request every time the MAC sublayer has a symbol to output. Once the MAC sublayer has sent a PH__DATA.request to the PHY layer, it may not send another PH__DATA.request until it has received a PH__DATA.confirmation from the PHY layer.

Effect of Receipt. Upon receipt of this primitive, the PHY entity shall encode and transmit the symbol. When the PHY entity is ready to accept another PH__DATA.request, it shall return to the MAC sublayer a PH__DATA.confirmation.

Additional Comments. None.

5.2.2.2 PH__DATA.indication. This primitive defines the transfer of data from the PHY layer to the MAC sublayer entity.

Semantics of the Service Primitive

PH__DATA.indication (
                    symbol
)

The symbol specified shall be one of the following:

    0 = binary zero
    1 = binary one
    J = non-data-J
    K = non-data-K

When Generated. The PHY layer shall send the MAC sublayer a PH__DATA.indication every time the PHY layer decodes a symbol. This indication is sent once every symbol period.

Effect of Receipt. Upon receipt of this primitive the MAC sublayer accepts a symbol from the PHY layer.

Additional Comments. None.

5.2.2.3 PH__DATA.confirmation. This primitive has local significance and shall provide an appropriate response to the MAC sublayer PH__DATA.request primitive signifying the acceptance of a symbol specified by the PH__DATA.request and willingness to accept another symbol.

Semantics of the Service Primitive

PH__DATA.confirmation (

transmission__status

)

The transmission__status parameter shall be used to signify the transmission completion status.

When Generated. The PHY layer shall send the MAC sublayer PH__DATA.confirmation in response to every PH__DATA.request received by the PHY layer. The purpose of the PH__DATA.confirmation is to synchronize the MAC sublayer data output with the data rate of the PHY layer medium.

Effect of Receipt. The receipt of this primitive enables the MAC sublayer to send another PH__DATA.request to the PHY layer.

Additional Comments. The PHY layer provides a *synchronous* service, that is, upon completion of a PH__DATA.confirmation, it expects an immediate PH__DATA.request.

5.3 MAC to NMT Service. This section specifies the services provided at the boundary between the network management and the MAC sublayer. This interface is used by NMT to monitor and control the operations of the MAC sublayer.

5.3.1 Interactions. The following primitives are defined for the NMT to request service from the MAC sublayer:

MA__INITIALIZE__PROTOCOL.request
MA__INITIALIZE__PROTOCOL.confirmation
MA__CONTROL.request
MA__STATUS.indication
MA__NMT__DATA.request
MA__NMT__DATA.indication
MA__NMT__DATA.confirmation

All primitives described in this section are mandatory.

5.3.2 Detailed Service Specifications. All primitives are specified in exemplary form only. Each service shall name the particular primitive and the required information that will be passed between the MAC sublayer and NMT.

5.3.2.1 MA__INITIALIZE__PROTOCOL.request. This primitive has local significance and is used by NMT to reset the MAC sublayer and optionally to change operational parameters of the MAC sublayer.

Semantics of the Service Primitive

MA__INITIALIZE__PROTOCOL.request
(
individual__MAC__address,
group__MAC__addresses,
all__stations__this__ring__address,
THT__value,
TRR__value,
TVX__value,
TNT__value,
TQP__value,
TSM__value,
TAM__value,
priority__of AMP__data__unit,
indicate__for__frame__with__SA=MA,
indicate__for__rcv__only__good__frames
)

(1) The individual__MAC__address is the octet string the MAC sublayer will use as its individual address.

(2) The group__MAC__addresses is the octet string the MAC sublayer will use as its group addresses.

(3) The all__stations__this__ring__address parameter is the octet string the MAC sublayer will use as the destination address in frames sent to all stations, this ring. This value will also be used to determine whether to copy a frame sent by another station with a destination address of all stations, this ring. The default value is all ones.

(4) The THT__value is the value the MAC sublayer will use for its Timer, Holding Token (THT).

(5) The TRR__value is the value the MAC sublayer will use for the time-out value of its Timer, Return to Repeat (TRR).

(6) The TVX__value is the value the MAC sublayer will use for the time-out value of its Timer, Valid Transmission (TVX).

(7) The TNT__value is the value the MAC sublayer will use for the time-out value of its Timer, No Token (TNT).

(8) The TQP__value is the value the MAC sublayer will use for the time-out value of its Timer, Queue PDU (TQP).

(9) The TSM__value is the value the MAC sublayer will use for the time-out value of its Timer, Standby Monitor (TSM).

(10) The TAM__value is the value the MAC sublayer will use for the time-out value of its Timer, Active Monitor (TAM).

(11) The priority__of__AMP__data__unit parameter is the value the MAC sublayer will use for the requested__service__class when sending the AMP data unit (see 3.3.3).

(12) The indicate_for_frame_with_SA=MA parameter is the value the MAC sublayer will use to initialize the station to generate MA_DATA.indication and MA_NMT_DATA.indication primitives for frames that the station itself transmitted (that is, SA=MA).

(13) The indicate_for_rcv_only_good_frames parameter is the value the MAC sublayer will use to decide whether to generate MA_DATA.indication and MA_NMT_DATA.indication primitives only on frames that are good (see 4.2.1) or alternatively on all frames that are validly formed. In both cases data is terminated when a bit synchronization error is recognized.

NOTE. All parameters of this primitive are optional. If a parameter is omitted, the MAC sublayer will use the most recently provided value for this parameter or if no value has been previously provided, the default value for the parameter will be used. The default value for the individual_MAC_address parameter is not defined here.

When Generated. This primitive shall be generated by NMT whenever NMT requires the MAC sublayer to reset and reconfigure.

Effect on Receipt. Receipt of this primitive shall cause the MAC sublayer to reset its protocol and establish the values of its addresses, timers, and other initialization parameters. Upon completion of this primitive, the MAC sublayer shall generate a MA_INITIALIZE_PROTOCOL.confirmation.

Additional Comments. The timer values specified by NMT to the MAC sublayer by this primitive, may effect the maximum length frame that LLC may request the MAC sublayer to transmit. It is the responsibility of NMT to inform the appropriate higher layers responsible for segmenting or blocking messages of the MAC sublayer maximum frame size.

5.3.2.2 MA_INITIALIZE_PROTOCOL.confirmation. This primitive is used by the MAC sublayer to inform NMT that the MA_INITIALIZE_PROTOCOL.request primitive is complete.

Semantics of the Service Primitive

MA_INITIALIZE_PROTOCOL.confirmation (

                                status

)

The status parameter indicates the success or failure of the MA_INITIALIZE_PROTOCOL.request.

When Generated. This primitive shall be generated by MAC upon completion of a MA_INITIALIZE_PROTOCOL.request.

Effect on Receipt. Unspecified.

Additional Comments. None.

5.3.2.3 MA_CONTROL.request. This primitive has local significance and is used by NMT to control the operation of the MAC sublayer.

Semantics of the Service Primitive

MA_CONTROL.request (

control_action

)

The control_action parameter shall be one of the following:
MASTER RESET (see 4.2.3)
INSERT (see 4.2.3)

When Generated. This primitive shall be generated by NMT whenever NMT requires the MAC sublayer to take specific actions.

Effect on Receipt. Receipt of this primitive shall cause the MAC sublayer to take the action specified by the control_action parameter.

Additional Comments. None

5.3.2.4 MA_STATUS.indication. This primitive is used by the MAC sublayer to inform NMT of errors and significant status changes. The specific errors and status changes reported are defined in the following section.

Semantics of the Service Primitive

MA_STATUS.indication (

status_report

)

The status_report parameter shall be one of the following:

FRAME_CONDITION. See Receive Actions reference R-A.
TX_CLAIM_TOKEN_STATE. See Standby Monitor FSM transitions 11, 41, 52.
TX_BEACON_STATE. See Standby Monitor FSM transitions 53.
RECEIVE_FRAME_BEACON. See Standby Monitor FSM transition 42A.
ENTER_ACTIVE_STATE. See Active Monitor FSM transition 11.
ENTER_STANDBY_STATE. See Active Monitor FSM transitions 04, 22, and Standby Monitor FSM transitions 22,31,51.
DUPLICATE_ADD_DETECTED. See Standby Monitor FSM transition 21 and Receive Actions reference R-G.

When Generated. This primitive shall be generated by the MAC sublayer by the operation of the Operational, Standby Monitor, or Active Monitor FSMs.

Effect on Receipt. Unspecified.

Additional Comments. None

5.3.2.5 MA__NMT__DATA.request. This primitive defines the transfer of data from a local NMT entity to the local MAC entity.

Semantics of the Service Primitive

MA__NMT__DATA.request (
> frame__control,
> destination__address,
> m__sdu,
> requested__service__class
>)

The frame__control parameter specifies the value for the frame's FC octet. The destination__address parameter may specify either an individual or a group MAC entity address. It shall contain sufficient information to create the DA field that is appended to the frame by the local MAC sublayer entity as well as any lower level address information. The m__sdu parameter specifies the MAC service data unit to be transmitted by the MAC sublayer entity. There is sufficient information associated with m__sdu for the MAC sublayer entity to determine the length of the data unit. The requested__service__class parameter specifies the priority (Pm) desired for the data unit transfer.

When Generated. This primitive shall be generated by the NMT entity whenever data must be transferred to one or more peer NMT entities.

Effect of Receipt. The receipt of this primitive shall cause the MAC entity to append all MAC specific fields, including DA, SA, and any fields that are unique to the particular medium access method, and pass the properly formed frame to the lower layers of protocol for transfer to the peer NMT entity or entities.

Additional Comments. Requested__service__class is one of 8 levels.

5.3.2.6 MA__NMT__DATA.indication. This primitive defines the transfer of data from the MAC sublayer entity to the NMT entity.

Semantics of the Service Primitive

MA__NMT__DATA.indication (
> frame__control,
> destination__address,
> source__address,
> m__sdu,
> reception__status
>)

The frame_control parameter is the FC octet received. The destination_address parameter may be either an individual or a group address as specified by the DA field of the incoming frame. The source_address parameter must be an individual address as specified by the SA field of the incoming frame. The m_sdu parameter shall specify the MAC service data unit as received by the local MAC entity. The reception_status parameter indicates the success or failure of the incoming frame. It consists of the following elements:

(1) frame_status: FR_GOOD, FR_WITH_ERROR.

If an FR_WITH_ERROR is reported, the reason for the error shall also be reported. The reason shall be one of the following:

(a) invalid_FCS: calculated FCS does not match the received FCS

(b) code_violation: J or K symbol received between the SD and ED

(c) frame_truncated: the received frame, although free from errors, exceeded the internal buffer space

(d) short_frame: the received frame was shorter than the minimum

(2) E_value: zero, one, invalid

(3) A_&_C_value: zero_zero, one_zero, one_one, invalid

When Generated. The MA_NMT_DATA.indication primitive shall be generated by the MAC sublayer entity to the NMT entity or entities to indicate the arrival of a MAC frame at the local MAC sublayer entity. Such frames shall be reported only if they are validly formed and their destination address designates the local MAC entity, or the source address designates the local MAC entity if the station was so initialized (see 5.3.2.1).

Effect of Receipt. The effect of receipt of this primitive by NMT is dependent upon the validity and content of the frame.

Additional Comments. If the local MAC sublayer entity is designated by the destination_address parameter of a MA_NMT_DATA.request primitive, the indication primitive shall also be invoked by the MAC entity to the local NMT entity. This full duplex characteristic of the MAC sublayer may be due to unique function capabilities within the MAC sublayer or full duplex characteristics of the lower layers (for example, frames transmitted to the broadcast address shall invoke MA_NMT_DATA.indication primitives at all stations in the network including the station that generated the request).

5.3.2.7 MA_NMT_DATA.confirmation. This primitive has local significance and shall provide an appropriate response to the NMT's MA_NMT_DATA.request primitive signifying the success or failure of the request.

Semantics of the Service Primitive

> MA__NMT__DATA.confirmation (
>
> > > transmission__status,
> > > provided__service__class
> > >)

The transmission__status parameter shall be used to pass status information back to the local requesting NMT entity. It shall be used to indicate the success or failure of the previous associated MA_DATA.request. The provided__service__class parameter specifies the service class that was provided for the data unit transfer.

When Generated. This primitive shall be generated by MAC in response to an MA__NMT__DATA.request from the local NMT entity.

Effect of Receipt. The effect of receipt of this primitive by the NMT is unspecified.

Additional Comments. It is assumed that sufficient information is available to the NMT entity to associate the response with the appropriate request.

5.4 PHY to NMT Service. The services provided by the PHY layer to NMT allow the local NMT to control the operation of the PHY layer.

5.4.1 Interactions. The following primitives are defined for the NMT to request services from the PHY layer

> PH__CONTROL.request
> PH__STATUS.indication

All primitives described in this section are mandatory.

5.4.2 Detailed Service Specifications. This primitive is specified in exemplary form only. The service shall name the primitive and specify the information that will be passed between PHY and NMT.

5.4.2.1 PH__CONTROL.request. This primitive shall be generated by NMT to request the PHY layer to insert or remove itself to/from the ring.

Semantics of the Service Primitives

> PH__CONTROL.request (
>
> > > control__action
> > >)

The control__action parameter shall be one of the following:

> INSERT: signal insertion into ring
> REMOVE: signal removal from ring

When Generated. This primitive shall be generated by NMT when NMT requires insertion or removal of the station from the ring.

Effect Upon Receipt. The PHY layer shall take appropriate action to cause insertion or removal from the ring. See 7.4 for specific actions for shielded twisted pair medium.

Additional Comments. None.

5.4.2.2 PH_STATUS.indication. This primitive is used by the PHY layer to inform NMT of errors and significant status changes. The specific errors and status changes reported are defined in the following section.

Semantics of the Service Primitives

PH_STATUS.indication (

status_report

)

The status_report parameter shall be one of the following:

BURST_CORRECTION_START. The PHY layer has begun generating 0 or 1 symbols and passing them to the MAC sublayer (on the PH_DATA.indication) to correct detected silence on the medium.
BURST_CORRECTION_END. The PHY layer has stopped generating symbols; transitions have again been detected on the medium.
LATENCY_BUFFER_OVERFLOW. The PHY layer has attempted to expand the latency buffer beyond 30 bits.
LATENCY_BUFFER_UNDERFLOW. The PHY layer has attempted to contract the latency buffer beyond 24 bits.

When Generated. This primitive shall be generated by the PHY layer by its operation, as defined in 6.1 and 6.5.

Effect Upon Receipt. Unspecified.

Additional Comments. None.

6. Physical Layer

The following sections define physical (PHY) layer specifications. These include data symbol encoding and decoding, symbol timing, and reliability.

Throughout this section the word *repeater* is used to mean the repeater part of a station or a separate unit.

6.1 Symbol Encoding. The PHY layer encodes and transmits the four symbols presented to it at its MAC interface by the MAC sublayer.

The symbols exchanged between the MAC and PHY layers are shown below. (Specific implementations are not constrained in the method of making this information available.)

    0 = binary zero
    1 = binary one
    J = non-data-J
    K = non-data-K

As shown in Fig 6-1, the symbols are transmitted to the medium in the form of differential Manchester-type coding which is characterized by the transmission of two line signal elements per symbol.

In the case of the two data symbols, binary one and binary zero, a signal element of one polarity is transmitted for one half the duration of the symbol to be transmitted, followed by the contiguous transmission of a signal element of the opposite polarity for the remainder of the symbol duration. This provides two distinct advantages:

(1) The resulting signal has no dc component and can readily be inductively or capacitively coupled

(2) The forced *mid-bit* transition conveys inherent timing information on the channel

In the case of differential Manchester coding, the sequence of line signal element polarities is completely dependent on the polarity of the trailing signal element of the previously transmitted data or non-data symbol (bit). If the symbol to be transmitted is a binary zero, the polarity of the leading signal element of the sequence is opposite to that of the trailing element of the previous symbol and, consequently, a transition occurs at the bit (symbol) boundary as well as mid-bit. If the symbol to be transmitted is a binary one, the algorithm is reversed and the polarity of the leading signal element is the same as that of the trailing signal element of the previous bit. Here there is no transition at the bit (symbol) boundary.

The non-data symbols, J and K, depart from the above rule in that a signal element of the same polarity is transmitted for both signal elements of the symbol and there is therefore no mid-bit transition. A J symbol has the same polarity as the preceding symbol whereas a K symbol has the opposite polarity to the preceding symbol. The transmission of only one non-data symbol introduces a dc component on the ring. To avoid an accumulating dc component,

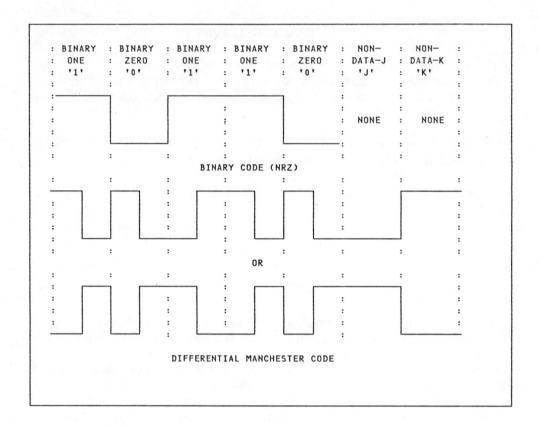

Fig 6-1
Example of Symbol Encoding

non-data symbols are normally transmitted as a pair of J and K symbols. (By its nature a K symbol is opposite to the polarity of the preceding symbol.)

6.2 Symbol Decoding. Received symbols shall be decoded using an algorithm that is the inverse of the one described for symbol encoding, and the decoded symbols shall be presented at the MAC interface.

If the PHY layer receives more than four signal elements of the same polarity in succession, it shall introduce a change of polarity (that is, a transition) at the end of the fourth signal element in the received bit stream and continue to introduce a transition each signal element time until a transition is received from the ring. The resulting bit stream is then decoded and the symbols presented to the MAC interface.

In a similar manner, during periods of loss of clock synchronization or underrun/overrun of the latency buffer, the PHY layer shall generate a transition each signal element time, decode the new bit stream, and present the resulting symbols to the MAC interface.

6.3 Data Signalling Rates. The data signalling rates shall be 1 or 4 Mbit/s with a tolerance of ±0.01%.

6.4 Symbol Timing. The PHY layer shall recover the symbol timing information inherent in the transitions between levels of the received signal. It shall minimize the phase jitter in this recovered timing signal to provide suitable timing at the data signalling rate for internal use and for the transmission of symbols on the ring. The rate at which symbols are transmitted is adjusted continuously in order to remain in phase with the receive signal.

In normal operation there is one station on the ring that is the active monitor. All other stations on the ring are frequency and phase locked to this station. They extract timing from the received data by means of a phase locked loop. The phase locked loop design shall be based on the following criteria:

(1) It shall limit the dynamic alignment jitter at any station in the ring to a 3 sigma value of 10°.

(2) Whenever a station is inserted into the ring or loses phase lock with the upstream station, it shall, upon receipt of a signal which is within specification from the upstream station (re)acquire phase lock within 1.5 ms.

(3) It shall accommodate at least a combined total of 250 stations and repeaters on the ring.

(4) It shall operate with a receive signal as specified in Section 7.

(5) It shall operate with a jitter power spectral density of $2.5 \cdot 10^{-25}$ s²/Hz, which may have been added by the medium interface cable and medium to the output of the upstream station.

NOTE: Items 1, 2, and 3 above require the design of the phase lock loop to meet the simultaneous requirements of large loop bandwidth to meet the 1.5 ms clock acquisition, and high damping to meet the 250 station capability. The loop transfer function must be designed to have a gain overshoot that is less than 0.2 dB above 0.0 dB.

6.5 Latency Buffer. The latency buffer is provided by the active monitor. It serves two distinct functions.

Assured Minimum Latency. In order for the token to continuously circulate around the ring when all stations are in repeat mode, the ring must have a latency (that is, time, expressed in number of bits transmitted, for a signal element to proceed around the entire ring) of at least the number of bits in the token sequence, that is, 24. Since the latency of the ring varies from one system to another and no a priori knowledge is available, a delay of at least 24 bits shall be provided by the active monitor.

Phase Jitter Compensation. The source timing or master oscillator of the ring shall be supplied by the active monitor station. All other stations in the ring track the frequency and phase of the incoming signal they receive. Although the mean data signalling rate around the ring is controlled by the active monitor station, segments of the ring can, instantaneously, operate at speeds slightly higher or lower than the frequency of the master oscillator. The cumulative effect of these variations in speed are sufficient to cause effective variations of up to $\pm$ 3 bits in the latency of a ring that has been configured with a maximum number of stations (that is, 250).

However, unless the latency of the ring remains constant, bits will be either dropped (not retransmitted) as the latency of the ring decreases or added as the latency increases. In order to maintain a constant ring latency, an elastic buffer with a length of 6 bits (12 signal elements) is added to the fixed 24-bit buffer. The resulting 30-bit buffer is initialized to 27 bits. If the received signal at the active monitor station is slightly faster than the master oscillator, the buffer will expand, as required, to 28, 29, or 30 bits to avoid dropping bits. If the received signal is slow, the buffer will contract to 26, 25, or 24 bits to avoid adding bits to the repeated bit stream.

7. Station Attachment Specifications— Shielded Twisted Pair

7.1 Scope. This section specifies the functional, electrical, and mechanical characteristics of balanced, baseband, shielded twisted pair attachment to the trunk cable of a token ring.

7.2 Overview. The function of the trunk cable medium is to transport data signals between successive stations of a baseband ring local area network. This communications medium consists of a set of TCU's interconnected sequentially by trunk cable links. Each TCU is connected to a TCU/MIC cable to which a station may be connected. The relationship between these embodiments and the LAN model are shown in Fig 7-1.

Repeaters may be used, where required, to extend the length of a trunk link beyond limits imposed by normal signal degradation due to link impairments. These repeaters serve to restore the amplitude, shape, and timing of signals passing through them. The repeater's regenerative functions have the same characteristics as a repeating station on the ring and must be included in the count of the number of stations supported by the ring.

Fig 7-1
Partitioning of the Physical Layer and Medium

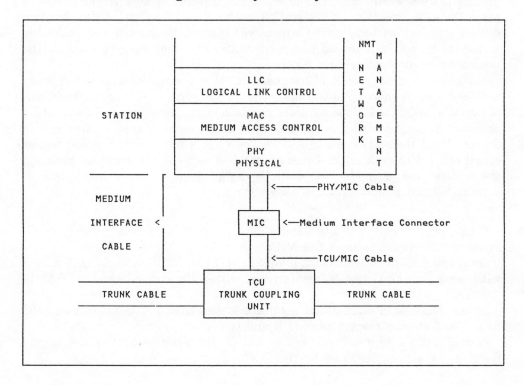

The medium interface cable (MIC) shown in Fig 7-1 may be as shown or may include multiple sections of cable joined by connectors identical to the MIC. By definition, the MIC is the connector at which all transmitted and received signal specifications shall be met. It may be attached to the station directly or on a *pig tail*.

7.3 Coupling of the Station to the Ring. The connection of the station to the trunk cable medium shall be via a shielded cable containing two balanced, 150 ± 15 Ω twisted pairs. The station transmitter shall deliver the specified signal at the MIC, and the station receiver shall have sufficient sensitivity and distortion margin to operate properly with the appearance of the specified signal levels and distortion at this interface point. The shield of the cables shall be connected to the shield terminal of the MIC.

An exemplary implementation of the connection, in bypass mode, of the station to the ring is shown in Fig 7-2.

7.4 Ring Access Control. Station insertion into the ring is controlled by the station. The mechanism for effecting the insertion or bypass of the station resides in the TCU. The station exercises control of the mechanism via the media interface cable using a phantom circuit technique. The phantom circuit impresses a dc voltage on the MIC. This dc voltage is transparent to the passage of station-transmitted symbols, hence the name *phantom*. The voltage impressed is used within the TCU to effect the transfer of a switching action to cause the serial insertion of the station in the ring. Cessation of the phantom drive causes a switching action which will bypass the station and cause the station to be put in a looped (*wrapped*) state. This loop may be used by the station for off-line self-testing functions.

The phantom drive circuit is designed such that the station may detect open-wire and certain short-circuit faults in either the receive pair or transmit pair of signal wires. This is done by detecting dc current imbalance in two separate phantom circuits. In order to do this the transformers (or their equivalent) in the TCU and the station must provide two coils which are dc isolated but ac signal coupled to each other. Circuits attached between the transmit pair and the receive pair of conductors shall be designed such that a line-to-line dc current balance is maintained within each pair.

7.4.1 Current and Voltage Limits. The point of measurement of the voltage and current limits is at the MIC.

Insertion shall be effected with a voltage of 4.1 to 7.0 V on MIC pin B and O with return on pin G and R, respectively, within the current range of 0.65 to 2.0 mA.

Bypass shall be effected when a voltage of less than 1 V is present on MIC pins B and O with respect to pins R and G.

A load with a dc resistance within 5% of the insertion/bypass mechanism resistance shall be presented by the TCU on pins G and O.

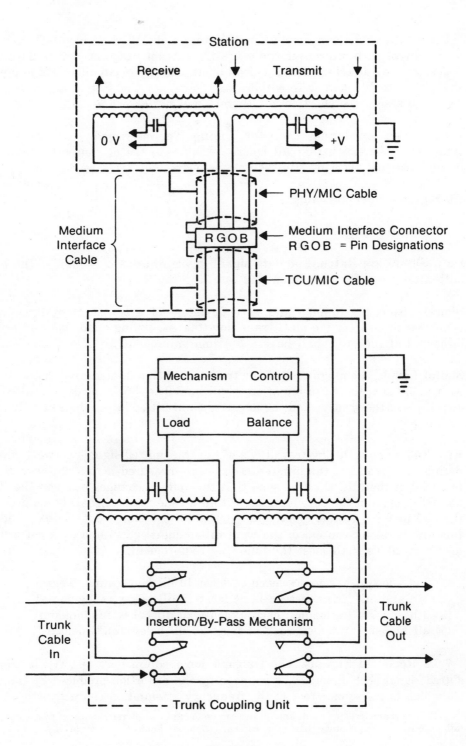

**Fig 7-2
Example of Station Connection to the Medium**

The operating voltage supplied by the station on MIC pins B and O shall be within 1% of each other over the operating current range of 0.65 to 2.0 mA.

The MIC, as described later, will automatically short circuit pin R to pin O and pin G to B when it is withdrawn. Therefore, the station shall provide means to assure the short circuit current will not exceed 20 mA.

7.4.2 Insertion/Bypass Transfer Timing. The insertion/bypass mechanism shall break the existing circuit before establishing the new circuit. The maximum time that the ring trunk circuit is open shall not exceed 5 ms.

7.5 Signal Characteristics

7.5.1 Transmitted Signals

Data Signalling Rates. The data signalling rates are 1 or 4 Mbit/s. The permitted tolerance for each signalling rate is ± 0.01%.

Signal Jitter. Maximum cumulative deviation of a transmitted signal element transition from the ideal transition (that is, timing distortion and *jitter*) measured at the MIC shall have a 3 sigma value of 10°.

Signal Level. The magnitude of the transmitted signal, measured at the MIC, with a 150 Ω resistive termination, shall be 3.0 to 4.5 V, peak to peak. The amplitude of the positive and the negative transmitted levels shall be balanced within 5%.

Rise/Fall Times. During transitions of the transmitted signals between alternating binary states, the differential voltage measured across a 150 ± 15 Ω test load at the MIC shall be such that the voltage changes between the 10% and 90% points of the output signal within a time interval shall be no greater than 25 ns for a 4 Mbit/s data rate (100 ns for a 1 Mbit/s data rate). In addition, the harmonic content of the transmitted signal generated by a pattern of all 0's or all 1's shall meet the following requirement:

(1) 2nd and 3rd harmonics: each at least 10 dB below fundamental
(2) 4th and 5th harmonics: each at least 15 dB below fundamental
(3) 6th and 7th harmonics: each at least 20 dB below fundamental
(4) all higher harmonics: each at least 25 dB below fundamental

7.5.2 Received Signals. The transmission medium may distort the transmitted signal. The distortion is bounded by the distortion produced by the cable which has a square root of the frequency attenuation characteristic.

(NOTE: This characteristic is well known and can be found in many reference text books. Specifically, the form of the characteristic is in *Reference Data for Radio Engineers* [4].[2]

---

[2]The numbers in brackets correspond to those in the references at the end of this section.

In addition, flat (non-distorting) attenuation may be caused by the medium, especially TCU's and connectors. The total attenuation may vary from 0 to 29 dB at 4 MHz (at 1 MHz for 1 Mbit/s data rate) including flat attenuation not exceeding 15 dB, and cable attenuation not exceeding 26 dB at 4 MHz (at 1 MHz for 1 Mbit/s data rate). The total allowable attenuation may be less than 29 dB based on the actual noise level at the MIC and the required error rate of the LAN. The error rate required of a LAN shall be established by mutual agreement among the users of the LAN but in no case shall it be less than 10^{-8}.

In order to specify meaningful measurements at the MIC, a measurement is outlined that, while not part of the specification, allows confirmation of system level conformance. All received signals and noise will be specified at the output of an equalizing filter. The filter is a 2-pole, 1-zero device. For 4 Mbit ring operation the filter shall have poles at 2.7 MHz and 16 MHz, and zero at 540 kHz, each with a tolerance of ±5%. (For 1 Mbit operation, the frequency points are all divided by 4.) A plot of the characteristics of the filter are shown in Fig 7-3.

Fig 7-3
Receive Filter Characteristics for 4 Mbit/s Operational
150 Ω Impedance

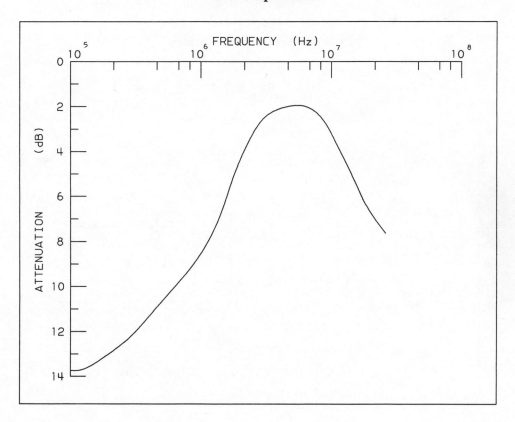

Signal Level. The receive signal at the output of the terminated filter shall have at least a magnitude of 25 mV during the central third of the half-bit time. Fig 7-4 is the characteristic *eye* pattern of the received signal when viewed on an oscilloscope triggered by a non-critical phase lock loop with a band width equal to or less than 0.01 times the data rate. A compliant signal shall have an opening such that a rectangular area of 50 mV high (2 × 25 mV) and a width of 33% of the half-bit time will fit, symmetrically, within the eye as shown in Fig 7-4.

Error Rate. The station shall provide an output with an error rate of $\leq 10^{-9}$ when the S/N (signal-to-noise ratio) at the output of the specified filter is ≥ 22 dB. S/N, measured in dB, is defined as 20 log ($\frac{1}{2}$ minimum eye height during the central third of the half-bit time divided by rms noise).

7.6 Reliability. The MAC, PHY layers, and connecting cable up to and including the MIC of each station shall be designed to minimize the probability of causing communication failure among other stations attached to the local network. The mean time to the occurrence of such a failure shall be at least one million hours of operation without requiring manual intervention to restore the network to operational status.

Fig 7-4
Receive Signal Eye Pattern

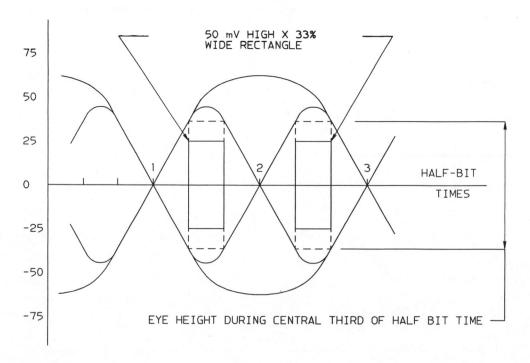

7.7 Safety and Grounding Requirements. All stations meeting this Standard shall conform to either IEC Standard 380 [2] or IEC Standard 435 [3].

All exposed materials shall meet appropriate flammability requirements. Low smoke and fume materials shall be used as mandated by local requirements.

7.8 Electromagnetic Susceptibility. Sources of interference from the environment include but are not limited to electromagnetic fields, electrostatic discharge, and transient voltages between earth connections.

The station hardware shall meet its specifications when operating in an ambient plane wave field of 2 V/m from 10 kHz to 30 MHz and 5 V/m from 30 MHz to 1 GHz.

7.9 Medium Interface Connector (MIC). Figure 7-5 shows an isometric view of the medium interface connector as it would be oriented when it is wall-mounted. It has four signal contacts with a ground contact and is hermaphroditic in design so that two identical units will mate when oriented 180° with respect to each other.

**Fig 7-5
Medium Interface Connector—Isometric View**

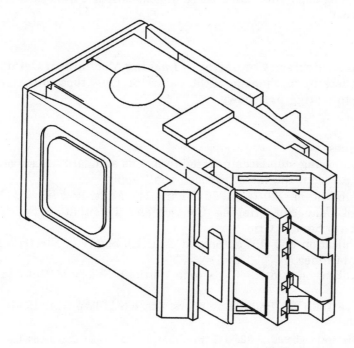

Electrical Characteristics

crosstalk rejection	> 62 dB @ 100 kHz to 4 MHz
connector insertion loss in a 150 Ω impedance line	< 0.1 dB @ 100 kHz to 4 MHz
dc contact resistance (connection according to IEC 130-14 [1])	
pins	20 mΩ average, 100 mΩ maximum
shield	25 mΩ average, 100 mΩ maximum
self-shorting path	40 mΩ average, 100 mΩ maximum
carry current	≥ 0.1 A
voltage proof contact-contact	≥ 750 V dc

Mechanical Characteristics

contact force	0.5 - 1.0 N
insertions	> 1000
life span	> 15 years
surface treatment (compatible with the following):	

    point-of-pin contact—plating with 3 μm of hard gold

    point-of-shield contact—plating with 5 μm of tin

7.9.1 Medium Interface Connector — Contactor Detail. Figure 7-6 shows the details of the signal and ground contractors. When the connector is disconnected, pin R shall be shorted to pin O and pin G shorted to pin B for automatic looping capability. Only those dimensions that are essential to mating are shown.

7.9.2 Medium Interface Connector — Locking Mechanism Detail. Figure 7-7 shows the locking mechanism of the connector. Only those dimensions that are essential to mating are shown.

7.10 References

When the following standards referred to in this standard are superseded by an approved revision, the latest revision shall apply.

[1] IEC Publication 130-14 (1975), Part 14, Multi-Row Board Mounted Printed Board Connectors Having Contact and Termination Spacing on a 2.54 mm (0.1 in) Square Grid.[3]

[2] IEC Publication 380 (1977) (Second Edition), Safety of Electrically Energized Office Machines.

[3] IEC Publication 435 (1983) (Second Edition), Safety of Data Processing Equipment.

[4] Reference Data for Radio Engineers, 4th ed, ITT, p 574, 1956.

---

[3]IEC Standards are available in the US from American National Standards Institute, 1430 Broadway, New York, NY 10018.

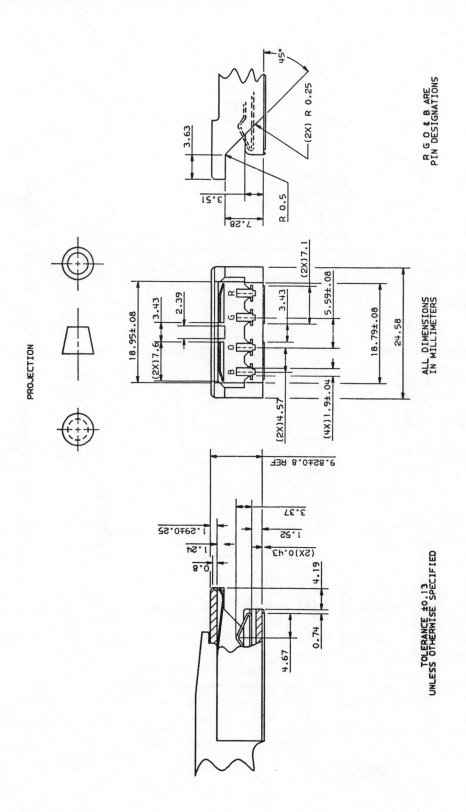

Fig 7-6
Medium Interface Connector — Contactor Detail

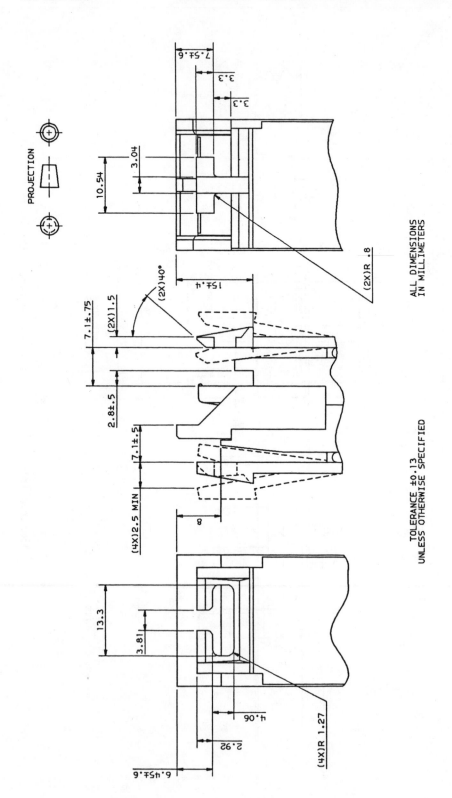

ALL DIMENSIONS
IN MILLIMETERS

TOLERANCE ±0.13
UNLESS OTHERWISE SPECIFIED

Fig 7-7
Medium Interface Connector — Locking Mechanism Detail

Appendix

Hierarchical Structuring for
Locally Administered Addresses

(This appendix is not a part of ANSI/IEEE Std 802.5-1985, Token Ring Access Method and Physical Layer Specifications, and is included for information only. The concepts introduced in this appendix are under study for inclusion in a future revision of this standard.)

A1. General Structure. The following structure provides for a token-ring LAN divided into multiple rings, with one or more MAC-level relay stations interconnecting the rings. Structuring MAC addresses in a hierarchical fashion can facilitate the operation of these relay stations.

A ring is defined as the collection of all stations of a LAN that have the same ring number and that can exchange frames without any intermediary MAC-level relay entity. Stations on a ring can communicate with stations with different ring numbers only through a MAC-level relay or some other intermediary.

A hierarchical address permits a MAC-level relay station to recognize frames that require forwarding to other rings by applying a straightforward algorithm to the frames to be forwarded.

The source and destination address partitioning recommended for this purpose is:

(1) 16-bit hierarchical form

I/G	7-bit ring number	8-bit station subaddress

(2) 48-bit locally administered hierarchical form

I/G	1	14-bit ring number	32-bit station subaddress

In addition to the definitions of broadcast address and null address, the following addressing conventions are recommended:

This ring. The ring number field is set to all 0's or to the ring number of this ring, if known.

All stations, this ring. The ring number field is set to all 0's or to the ring number of this ring, if known; the station subaddress field is set to all 1's.

All rings. The ring number field is set to all 1's.

A2. Group Addressing Modes. Two formats for group addressing are defined within the structure of hierarchical addressing (as described above), using the first bit of the station subaddress field:

0 = bit-significant mode
1 = conventional group mode

Bit-significant mode. Specifies that each bit in the station subaddress field represents a single group address. For 16-bit addresses, 7 bit-significant addresses may be defined in this mode; for 48-bit addresses, 31 bit-significant addresses may be defined.

Stations that are to copy frames destined for many different functions may implement a bit-significant mask to facilitate the copying of frames with bit-significant destination addresses. Such a mask could have a bit set to 1 for each bit-significant address for which the station wishes to copy frames. For example:

Function 'K' has bit-significant address B'0010000'.
Function 'P' has bit-significant address B'0000010'.

Ring station 'Y' has bit-significant mask B'0010010', implying that station Y can copy frames destined for both functions K and P.

Conventional group mode. Specifies that the remaining bits in the station subaddress field represent a single group address. For 16-bit addresses, this allows about $2^{**}7$ (127) group addresses in conventional group mode; for 48-bit addresses, this allows about $2^{**}31$ group addresses in conventional group mode.

The four options are illustrated below.

(1) 16-bit hierarchical form, bit-significant mode

1	7-bit ring number	0	up to 7 bit-significant addresses

(2) 48-bit locally administered hierarchical form, bit-significant mode

1	1	14—bit ring number	0	up to 31 bit—significant addresses

(3) 16-bit hierarchical form, conventional group mode

1	7—bit ring number	1	7—bit conventional group address

(4) 48-bit locally administered hierarchical form, conventional group mode

1	1	14—bit ring number	1	31—bit conventional group address